Solar Renewable Energy Certificate (SREC) Markets: Status and Trends

National Renewable Energy Laboratory (NREL)

This work has been selected by scholars as being culturally important, and is part of the knowledge base of civilization as we know it. This work was reproduced from the original artifact, and remains as true to the original work as possible. Therefore, you will see the original copyright references, library stamps (as most of these works have been housed in our most important libraries around the world), and other notations in the work.

This work is in the public domain in the United States of America, and possibly other nations. Within the United States, you may freely copy and distribute this work, as no entity (individual or corporate) has a copyright on the body of the work.

As a reproduction of a historical artifact, this work may contain missing or blurred pages, poor pictures, errant marks, etc. Scholars believe, and we concur, that this work is important enough to be preserved, reproduced, and made generally available to the public. We appreciate your support of the preservation process, and thank you for being an important part of keeping this knowledge alive and relevant.

NREL
NATIONAL RENEWABLE ENERGY LABORATORY

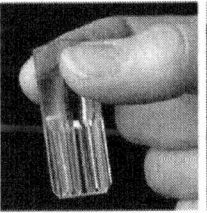

Solar Renewable Energy Certificate (SREC) Markets: Status and Trends

Lori Bird, Jenny Heeter, and Claire Kreycik

NREL is a national laboratory of the U.S. Department of Energy, Office of Energy Efficiency & Renewable Energy, operated by the Alliance for Sustainable Energy, LLC.

Technical Report
NREL/TP-6A20-52868
November 2011

Contract No. DE-AC36-08GO28308

≈NREL
NATIONAL RENEWABLE ENERGY LABORATORY

Solar Renewable Energy Certificate (SREC) Markets: Status and Trends

Lori Bird, Jenny Heeter, and Claire Kreycik

Prepared under Task No. SM10.2464

NREL is a national laboratory of the U.S. Department of Energy, Office of Energy Efficiency & Renewable Energy, operated by the Alliance for Sustainable Energy, LLC.

National Renewable Energy Laboratory
1617 Cole Boulevard
Golden, Colorado 80401
303-275-3000 • www.nrel.gov

Technical Report
NREL/TP-6A20-52868
November 2011

Contract No. DE-AC36-08GO28308

NOTICE

This report was prepared as an account of work sponsored by an agency of the United States government. Neither the United States government nor any agency thereof, nor any of their employees, makes any warranty, express or implied, or assumes any legal liability or responsibility for the accuracy, completeness, or usefulness of any information, apparatus, product, or process disclosed, or represents that its use would not infringe privately owned rights. Reference herein to any specific commercial product, process, or service by trade name, trademark, manufacturer, or otherwise does not necessarily constitute or imply its endorsement, recommendation, or favoring by the United States government or any agency thereof. The views and opinions of authors expressed herein do not necessarily state or reflect those of the United States government or any agency thereof.

Available electronically at http://www.osti.gov/bridge

Available for a processing fee to U.S. Department of Energy
and its contractors, in paper, from:

> U.S. Department of Energy
> Office of Scientific and Technical Information
> P.O. Box 62
> Oak Ridge, TN 37831-0062
> phone: 865.576.8401
> fax: 865.576.5728
> email: mailto:reports@adonis.osti.gov

Available for sale to the public, in paper, from:

> U.S. Department of Commerce
> National Technical Information Service
> 5285 Port Royal Road
> Springfield, VA 22161
> phone: 800.553.6847
> fax: 703.605.6900
> email: orders@ntis.fedworld.gov
> online ordering: http://www.ntis.gov/help/ordermethods.aspx

Cover Photos: (left to right) PIX 16416, PIX 17423, PIX 16560, PIX 17613, PIX 17436, PIX 17721

Printed on paper containing at least 50% wastepaper, including 10% post consumer waste.

Acknowledgments

The authors would like to thank Jennifer DeCesaro of the U.S. Department of Energy Solar Technologies Program for her support of this work. The authors would also like to thank the following individuals for reviewing this report: Brad Bowery of SRECTrade; Charlie Coggeshall of New West Technologies, LLC; Jennifer DeCesaro of DOE; Galen Barbose of Lawrence Berkeley National Laboratory; Dan Yonkin and Yuri Horwitz of Sol Systems; and Karlynn Cory, David Feldman, and Robin Newmark of NREL. We also wish to thank Mary Lukkonen of NREL and PWT Communications for editorial support. Finally, we wish to thank the following individuals for reviewing and providing information about their state solar requirements and SREC markets:

- Delaware: Courtney Stewart, Delaware Public Service Commission
- District of Columbia: Roger Fujihara, DC Public Service Commission
- Maryland: Kevin Mosier, Maryland Public Service Commission
- Massachusetts: Howard Bernstein, Mike Judge, and Natalie Andrews, Massachusetts Department of Energy Resources
- Missouri: Michael Taylor, Missouri Public Service Commission
- New Hampshire: Kate Epsen, New Hampshire Public Utilities Commission
- North Carolina: Sam Watson, North Carolina Utilities Commission
- Ohio: Stuart Siegfried, Anne Goodge, Mark Bellamy, Katie Johnson, and Kristin Braun, Public Utilities Commission of Ohio
- Pennsylvania: Scott Gebhardt and Matt Wurst, Pennsylvania Public Utility Commission.

List of Acronyms

AC	alternating current
ACP	alternative compliance payment
BTU	British thermal unit
AC	alternating current
DC	direct current
EDC	electric distribution company
EGS	electric generation supplier
EY	energy year
IOU	investor-owned utility
kW	kilowatts
MW	megawatts
MWh	megawatt-hour
PJM	Pennsylvania New Jersey Maryland Interconnection
PSC	public service commission
PUC	public utility commission
PV	photovoltaic
RFP	request for proposal
RPS	renewable portfolio standard
SREC	solar renewable energy certificate
W	Watt

Executive Summary

Solar renewable energy certificates (SRECs) represent the generation attributes of solar energy systems and can be traded separately from commodity electricity. A SREC is created for each megawatt-hour of electricity generated from solar energy systems. SREC markets have emerged in nine U.S. states and Washington, D.C., as a method to meet compliance with solar carve out provisions of renewable energy portfolio standards (RPS). Solar carve out provisions set requirements for solar generation or capacity. This report examines the status and trends of SREC markets. Key issues and trends discussed in the report include:

- SREC markets are relatively young but expected to grow rapidly in coming years as state solar requirements ramp up. New Jersey has been the dominant market for SREC trading to date, but SREC markets in other states are expanding. Nationwide, solar carve outs in SREC markets are scheduled to grow from more than 520 MW$_{AC}$ in 2011 to nearly 7,300 MW$_{AC}$ in 2025.

- Policymakers establish key elements when designing SREC policies. Some states allow solar thermal to participate in SREC markets, but overall the SREC market is dominated by solar photovoltaics (PV). In terms of geographic eligibility, several states limit eligibility to in-state development, while a few allow SRECs from a broader geographic region.

- Solar alternative compliance payments (ACPs) generally set a ceiling on prices and are scheduled to decline over time, reflecting expectations of declining PV costs. In shortage situations, SRECs typically trade near the solar ACP.

- Lack of long-term contracts has been a barrier to project developers obtaining financing in some markets. This issue may continue to be a problem particularly in areas where rebates or other supplemental incentives expire and SRECs become the primary incentive stream for financing systems. Several states have instituted provisions such as long-term contracting requirements, price floors, or standardized long-term contracts to try to overcome these challenges.

- Rate caps exist in some form in five SREC markets but have not been reached or are yet to be evaluated. The modest size of most solar carve outs suggests that it is not likely that rate caps will be reached in the near term.

- SREC markets are supporting a mix of PV system sizes, including residential, non-residential, and utility-scale systems. In most markets, about two-thirds of registered projects are smaller than 10 kW. Projects larger than 250 kW dominate capacity installed in a few markets, including North Carolina, Massachusetts, and New Jersey. There has been a trend toward large-sized projects in recent years.

- Compliance has proved challenging in a number of SREC markets in recent years, but adequate supplies are expected going forward in many of these regions. A handful of states reported compliance shortfalls in 2009. The first compliance periods for a few markets occurred in 2010 or 2011. Recently, SREC spot prices have leveled or decreased in a number of markets as supplies have increased and compliance challenges have eased.

- SREC markets are expected to grow to more than 4,300 MW by 2020. In the near term, a sharp drop in SREC prices indicates that some markets may be oversupplied. An increase in installations has occurred in the last year due to a greater focus on U.S. markets, in large part due to slower growth in Europe, as well as a substantial drop in module prices. Capacity growth has been fueled in part by the approaching end of the Federal Treasury 1603 cash grant program, which will expire at the end of 2011. Looking forward, the largest markets to date are expected to slow over the next year or two but others are expected to continue to expand in the interim.

Table of Contents

List of Figures viii

List of Tables viii

1   Introduction 1

2   SREC Market Overview and Design 2
    2.1   Market Size and Scope.. 2
    2.2   System Eligibility: PV and Solar Thermal... 5
    2.3   State and Regional Eligibility Rules Define Markets 7
    2.4   Solar Alternative Compliance Payment Levels 8
    2.5   Measurement and Verification Methods for SRECs 10
    2.6   Long-Term Contracting and Financing Provisions.. 12
    2.7   Rate Caps 17

3   SREC Market Trends 19
    3.1   Trading Volumes and Market Activity 19
    3.2   In-State Versus Out-of-State Sourcing 21
    3.3   Size of Systems Supplying SRECs 25
    3.4   SREC Prices 30
    3.5   Compliance in SREC Markets 32

4   Future Outlook 35

5   Summary and Conclusions 38

References 40

Appendix 47
   Long-Term Contracting Provisions: SREC Auctions in New Jersey 47
   Long-Term Contracting Provisions: Competitive Solicitations in Pennsylvania 48
   SREC Price Floor Programs: Massachusetts and New Jersey Utility PSE&G 48

List of Figures

Figure 1. Map of states with SREC markets 2
Figure 2. Future capacity required in SREC markets (2011–2025) 4
Figure 3. Solar alternative compliance payment levels over time 10
Figure 4. SRECs issued in PJM-GATS, 2010 19
Figure 5. Monthly SREC trading volumes in PJM-GATS, 2009–2011 21
Figure 6. (a) Source of SRECs retired for 2010 compliance in Maryland (b) Source of SRECs retired for 2010 compliance in Washington, D.C. 24
Figure 7. (a) Source of SRECs retired for 2010 compliance in Pennsylvania (b) Source of SRECs retired for 2010 compliance in Ohio 24
Figure 8. Number of PV projects by size and jurisdiction 26
Figure 9. Aggregate capacity (in MW) of registered PV projects by size and jurisdiction 26
Figure 10. Number and average size of facilities >250 kW installed annually in PJM-GATS 28
Figure 11. Aggregate capacity of utility scale (>1 MW) PV projects (completed and under development) 29
Figure 12. SREC spot prices (per MWh), August 2009 to September 2011 30
Figure 13. New Jersey solar carve out compliance 32
Figure 14. Average PV installed price Q1 2010 through Q2 2011 35
Figure 15. Capacity installed by month in New Jersey 37

List of Tables

Table 1. State SREC Policy Overview 3
Table 2. Capacity Required in SREC Markets (in MW_{AC}) 4
Table 3. Technologies Eligible to Participate in SREC Markets 6
Table 4. Geographic Eligibility Requirements in SREC Markets 7
Table 5. State Solar Alternative Compliance Payments 10
Table 6. State Requirements for Verifying Solar Output to Sell SRECs 11
Table 7. Rate Cap on RPS or Solar Set-Aside 17
Table 8. PV Capacity Additions (Annual and Cumulative) 20
Table 9. In-State Versus Out-of-State Project Registration as of October 2011 22
Table 10. New Jersey EDC Solicitation 10-Year Contract Pricing, 2011 31
Table 11. Pennsylvania EDC Solicitation Contract Pricing, 2010–2011 31
Table 12. State Solar Carve Out Compliance, 2007–2009 33

1 Introduction

Solar renewable energy certificate (SREC) markets have emerged in a number of U.S. states to encourage the adoption of solar energy systems. SRECs represent the generation attributes of solar energy systems and can be traded separately from commodity electricity. A SREC is created for each megawatt-hour (MWh) of electricity generated from solar energy systems. SREC markets have emerged in some U.S. states that have renewable portfolio standards (RPS). These standards require utilities or load-serving entities (LSEs) to procure minimum amounts of renewable energy, including solar energy, to serve their electricity loads. Obligated entities demonstrate compliance with RPS solar energy requirements by retiring SRECs that they have acquired from the market.

RPS policies are widespread in the United States. By June 2011, 29 states, Washington, D.C., and Puerto Rico had adopted RPS policies, while another eight states had renewable portfolio goals. Of the jurisdictions with RPS policies in place, 17 had adopted specific targets, or "RPS carve outs," for solar energy or distributed energy resources to ensure that these sources would be part of the resource mix (Wiser et al. 2010). More than half of the 17 jurisdictions with solar carve outs in their RPS allow the use of SRECs to demonstrate compliance with solar targets. Other states have relied on financial incentives such as grants, rebates, performance-based incentives, feed-in tariffs, or standard offer contracts to achieve solar requirements or goals. In many cases, these financial incentives are used in conjunction with SRECs to help achieve compliance with solar carve outs.

SREC markets are relatively new. New Jersey was the first state to rely heavily on SRECs as a market mechanism to meet its solar carve out. New Jersey's first compliance year with its carve out was 2005, and initially, New Jersey established a rebate program to incentivize systems. Due to the high cost and constraints on the state budget, the state switched to a market-based SREC program in 2007 (Hart 2010). Since then, some states in the mid-Atlantic and surrounding regions have used SRECs to enable obligated entities to meet their solar carve outs, sometimes with other support schemes as well.

In several western states, SRECs are used to track compliance with solar carve outs, but there is no active trading market. In some cases, SRECs may be sold into voluntary markets in which consumers, businesses, and institutions purchase the renewable energy equivalent of their electricity needs. However, SRECs have played a limited role in these markets to date.

This paper examines experience in SREC markets in the United States. It describes how SREC markets function—key policy design provisions, eligible technologies, state and regional eligibility rules, solar alternative compliance payments (ACPs), measurement and verification methods, long-term contracting provisions, and rate caps. It also examines the trends of SREC markets—trading volumes, sourcing trends, trends in the size of solar photovoltaic (PV) systems driven by these markets, and trends in price and compliance. Throughout, the paper explores key issues and challenges facing SREC markets and attempts by policymakers to address some of these market barriers. Data and information presented in this report are derived from SREC tracking systems, brokers and auctions, published reports, and information gleaned from market participants and interviews with state regulators responsible for SREC market implementation. The last section summarizes key findings.

2 SREC Market Overview and Design

2.1 Market Size and Scope
SREC Markets Have Expanded to 10 Jurisdictions

SREC markets have emerged or are in the early stages of implementation in 10 jurisdictions. While 17 jurisdictions have an RPS carve out requiring electricity providers to obtain a certain fraction of their generation portfolio from solar, distributed generation (DG), or customer-sited sources, not all of these states allow the use of SRECs for compliance. Figure 1 details the states that have an RPS solar carve out, and of those, which allow SREC trading.

Figure 1. Map of states with SREC markets

Trading in SRECs is relatively new. SREC markets began when state solar targets took effect in New Jersey and Pennsylvania in 2005 and in Delaware and Washington, D.C., in 2007 (see Table 1). SREC trading increased substantially in 2007 when New Jersey shifted from a rebate program to greater reliance on SREC markets to support solar projects. Since then, Maryland (2008), Ohio (2009), North Carolina (2010), New Hampshire (2010), and Massachusetts (2010) have begun implementation of their solar carve outs and associated SREC markets. Missouri's solar requirement took effect in 2011.

SREC targets vary considerably depending on the goals of each jurisdiction. The ultimate target for the percent of retail sales that must be met by solar energy varies from 0.2% by 2018 in North Carolina to a high of 3.5% by 2026 in Delaware (see Table 1 and Figure 1). If converted to a percentage of retail sales, New Jersey's target is even higher. The stringency of the solar target, as well as other policy features, determines the extent to which new solar development is encouraged.

Table 1. State SREC Policy Overview

State	Initial compliance year	Target (% of Retail Sales)	Obligated Entities
DC	2007	2.5% by 2023	All EDCs and EGSs
DE	2007	3.5% by EY 2026	All EDCs Municipals/co-ops can set their own comparable RPS schedule by 2013
MA	2010	400 MW PV*	All EDCs and EGSs
MD	2008	2% by 2022	All EDCs and EGSs, municipals, co-ops
MO	2011	0.3% by 2021	All IOUs**
NC	2010	0.2% by 2018	All IOUs, municipals, co-ops
NH	2010	0.3% by 2014	All IOUs and retail suppliers, excluding municipals
NJ	2005	5,316 GWh by EY 2026	All EDCs and EGSs
OH	2009	0.5% by 2024	All EDCs and EGSs
PA	2005	0.5% by 2021	All EDCs and EGSs, voluntary participation by municipals, co-ops

Source: DSIRE 2011a.
Note: EY = energy year; EGS = electric generation supplier; EDC = electric distribution company; IOU = investor-owned utility
*Massachusetts's target is adjusted based on market conditions during previous years. In 2010, the compliance obligation was 34,164 MWh, the generation equivalent of 30 MW of capacity operating at a 13% capacity factor. This is equivalent to 0.07% of retail sales.
** Empire District Electric, one of Missouri's four IOUs, is exempt from the state's solar energy standard because it installed renewable energy capacity equal to 15% of the utility's total owned fossil-fired generating capacity by January 2009 (DSIRE 2011a).

In terms of total megawatts required under SREC policies, New Jersey is by far the largest market, requiring approximately 319 MW_{AC} of solar capacity in 2011 and projected to have more than 4,000 MW_{AC} by 2025 (see
Table 2 and Figure 2). The next largest near-term markets are Massachusetts, Pennsylvania, and Ohio. The Maryland market, while relatively modest in 2011, has aggressive targets that would require it to increase rapidly, making it the fourth largest market by 2015 and second largest market after New Jersey in 2020.

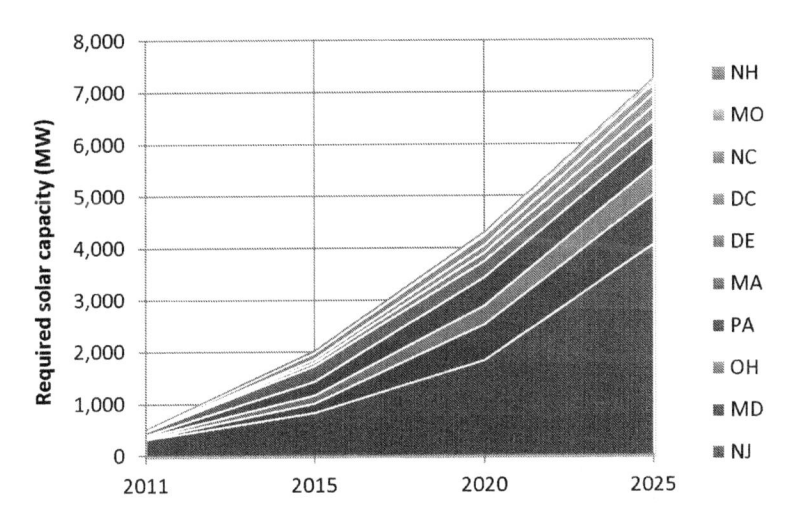

Figure 2. Future capacity required in SREC markets (2011–2025)

Source: Barbose 2011, with updates

Table 2. Capacity Required in SREC Markets (in MW$_{AC}$)

State	2011	2015	2020	2025
DC	>3	63	146	240
DE	10	69	162	261
MA	69	299	312	312
MD	22	179	693	958
MO	11	28	59	93
NC	18	121	181	190
NH	6	22	23	24
NJ	319	829	1,825	4,053
OH	31	155	363	553
PA	33	264	546	567
TOTAL	>522	2,029	4,310	7,251

Source: Barbose 2011, with updates.
Note: Most states have annual targets based on a percentage of retail electric sales in the compliance year. These estimates use the megawatt-hour target and convert it to megawatts using default capacity factors in NREL's PVWatts model, which determines the energy production of grid-connected PV systems. The capacity factors used assume that systems are south-facing and that the tilt is equal to the latitude of the state. The Massachusetts ultimate target, while not based on a percent of retail sales, requires a cumulative installment of 400 MW$_{DC}$ of solar capacity. These figures assume that Massachusetts's solar requirement are not adjusted for under- or over-supply.
Note: In Washington, D.C., the 2011 compliance obligation is uncertain because contracts entered into before July 12, 2011, are exempt from the District's increased solar requirement. This analysis assumes that existing contracts will expire before 2015 (Council of the District of Columbia 2011).

SREC markets began in restructured[1] states in the mid-Atlantic and Northeast but have since expanded into states with regulated electricity markets. In restructured states, where organized electricity markets are in place, multiple LSEs may need to procure SRECs to meet RPS requirements. The responsibility of satisfying the RPS requirements is placed on both electricity distribution companies (EDCs) that supply default service to customers and alternative suppliers, known as electricity generation suppliers (EGSs). In these markets, SRECs have been a useful tool. They enable trading among parties and they enable EGSs to procure SRECs from the spot market on a short-term basis or bi-laterally on a long-term basis. This flexibility of acquiring SRECs is important to both EDCs and EGSs because of uncertainty in future loads due to retail choice.

Several states with traditionally regulated electric utilities, including Missouri and North Carolina, allow the use of SRECs to achieve compliance with RPS targets. This enables utilities to procure SRECs from a broader geographic region than the state or balancing area. In a few states, municipal utilities and electric cooperatives are also obligated (or encouraged) to comply with RPS standards (see Table 1), in some cases with different targets.[2]

States measure RPS and solar set-aside compliance by looking at SRECs retired by the obligated entities. SRECs are retired when the owner designates that the SRECs will be used for compliance with a particular state RPS and transfers the SRECs to a retirement subaccount in the tracking system used to verify compliance. Regulators consider a 12-month span referred to as an energy year (EY) or compliance year. For example, the 2010 compliance period may consider SRECs retired between January 1, 2010, and December 31, 2010, or June 1, 2009, to May 31, 2010. Delaware, New Jersey, and Pennsylvania use a June 1 to May 31 period, while D.C., Maryland, Massachusetts, New Hampshire, North Carolina, and Ohio use a January 1 to December 31 period (SRECTrade 2011a).

2.2 System Eligibility: PV and Solar Thermal
SREC Market is Dominated by PV, Although Solar Thermal Is Eligible in Some States

A key policy design feature of solar carve outs that impacts SREC markets is technology eligibility. PV is an eligible—and most commonly used—technology in meeting solar carve out requirements in all SREC markets. Eligibility of solar thermal technologies is more varied.

About half of the state SREC markets allow solar thermal systems to participate (Table 3). Maryland, North Carolina, Ohio, and Washington, D.C., allow solar thermal technologies, including solar water heating, space heating and cooling systems, and other applications to

---

[1] In states that have undergone electricity market restructuring, electricity customers have retail choice, meaning that they can shop among electricity suppliers. EDCs own the distribution infrastructure and are the providers of last resort. EGSs are suppliers that have entered the market to provide electricity generation service.

[2] Publicly owned utilities are obligated in Maryland, while they are encouraged to comply voluntarily in Pennsylvania (UCS 2008) and can opt out of the Delaware RPS and solar set-aside if they create their own RPS standard by 2013. In North Carolina, a traditionally regulated electric market, investor-owned utilities (IOUs), municipal utilities, and electric cooperatives are required to meet the solar electricity requirement, though their overall RPS targets vary (12.5% for IOUs and 10% for munis/co-ops).

participate in the SREC market. Solar thermal systems in Delaware, Missouri, and Ohio must generate electricity in order to be eligible.[3] In Pennsylvania, solar thermal that generates electricity is eligible for the primary resource targets of Pennsylvania's RPS, but it is not eligible for the state's solar carve out.

Despite its eligibility in a number of states, solar thermal has played a limited role in SREC markets to date. Based on interviews with state regulators, few solar thermal projects have been used in SREC markets in Missouri, Ohio, and Washington, D.C. As of October 2011, 287 solar thermal projects have been registered in PJM-GATS; the majority of systems (75%) are located in Virginia and North Carolina (PJM-GATS 2011a). For example, in North Carolina, the public utilities commission had approved 50 solar thermal projects, primarily solar hot water systems, compared to 205 PV projects (NCUC 2011a).

Table 3. Technologies Eligible to Participate in SREC Markets

State	Solar PV	Solar Thermal
DC	Yes	Yes
DE	Yes	Yes, but must generate electricity
MA	Yes	No
MD	Yes	Solar water heating, but must be installed on or after June 1, 2011
MO	Yes	Yes, but must generate electricity
NC	Yes	Yes*
NH	Yes	No**
NJ	Yes	No
OH	Yes	Yes, but must generate electricity
PA	Yes	No***

Source: SRECTrade 2011a
* Eligible solar thermal resources include solar hot water, solar absorption cooling, solar dehumidification, solar thermally driven refrigeration, and solar industrial process heat.
** Solar water heating that displaces electricity is eligible for Class I of New Hampshire's RPS (Epsen 2011).
*** Solar thermal is eligible for Tier 1 of Pennsylvania's RPS.

States have expanded eligibility for use of solar thermal over time, indicating that there may be more development of solar thermal in the future. In December 2010, under the "Solar Collector Certification Temporary Amendment Act of 2010," the Washington, D.C., SREC market was expanded to include non-residential solar thermal systems, whereas previously only residential solar thermal systems were eligible. In May 2011, Maryland passed legislation enabling solar water heating systems to be eligible in the Maryland SREC market. Systems installed on or after June 1, 2011, are eligible.

---

[3] Solar thermal is also eligible to meet solar set-aside targets in states that do not use SRECs. These states include Arizona, Nevada, and New York (Wiser et al. 2010).

2.3 State and Regional Eligibility Rules Define Markets
Geographic Eligibility Requirements Influence the Location of Development

Another key policy design feature of solar carve outs that impacts SREC markets is limitations on the geographic eligibility of systems. Table 4 summarizes state geographic eligibility rules. Some jurisdictions limit the eligibility of solar to in-state projects through interconnection or other requirements (Delaware, Massachusetts, and New Jersey), while others allow a portion of the projects to come from out of state (North Carolina and Ohio). Other states allow SRECs sourced from projects in a specified region, such as the electric balancing area (Pennsylvania), or allow regional resources if in-state resources are insufficient (Maryland, though a binding in-state requirement goes into effect after 2011) (DSIRE 2011b). Washington, D.C., previously allowed regional resources to be used if local resources were insufficient; however, legislation enacted in August 2011 specifies that solar generating systems must be located within D.C. or in locations served by a distribution feeder serving D.C. Missouri is unique in that 100% of its solar standard can be met with SRECs from anywhere in the United States. North Carolina allows SRECs from anywhere in the United States to meet up to 25% of its solar carve out.

Table 4. Geographic Eligibility Requirements in SREC Markets

State	Geographic Eligibility
DC	In-district or in locations served by a distribution feeder serving the District
DE	Customer-sited solar must be located in state; non-customer sited solar can be located with PJM, or show import capabilities into PJM
MA	In state
MD	Solar resources must be connected with the distribution grid serving Maryland. On or before December 31, 2011, solar resources not connected to the Maryland grid are eligible if electricity suppliers were unable to contract for in-state SRECs
MO	Out-of-state eligible (anywhere)
NC	25% from out-of-state eligible (anywhere)
NH	Within New England or New York
NJ	In state
OH	50% of SRECs must be generated by in-state resources; bordering states (DC, IN, KY, MD, MI, PA, WV) and areas able to prove delivery to Ohio are eligible for 50%
PA	Out-of-state eligible (within PJM)

Source: DSIRE 2011a, Epsen 2011

Because only a few states allow SRECs to come from a broad geographic region, the national market for SRECs is limited. Generally, for nationally sourced SRECs to be eligible to qualify for RPS compliance, systems must be registered in renewable energy certificate (REC) tracking systems. For example, California and other western states have supplied SRECs registered in the Western Renewable Energy Generation Information System (WREGIS) tracking system to North Carolina and Missouri to help meet their solar requirements. There are currently nine REC tracking systems in operation in the United States.

In California, the state with the most grid-connected PV capacity, system owners retain the RECs and can resell them into SREC markets, even if they receive financial incentives under the California Solar Initiative.[4] The California Public Utilities Commission has issued a proposed decision that would allow system owners who install PV systems under the California Solar Initiative program to sell their SRECs to California utilities to meet the portion of the new 33% by 2020 RPS that can be met with RECs (CPUC 2011).

Some states have faced challenges regarding RPS geographic eligibility rules on the basis of the Dormant Commerce Clause of the U.S. Constitution, which precludes states from discriminating against or impeding interstate commerce. For example, Massachusetts faced a Commerce Clause challenge to its solar requirement, resulting in a partial settlement whereby the in-state requirement remains in place with modifications to its solar price cap, or solar alternative compliance payment (ACP), mechanism among other changes (Elefant and Holt 2011). However, in-state solar or DG requirements are untested by the courts to date.

The design of geographic restrictions may have bearing on the constitutionality. According to a recent legal analysis, solar or DG carve outs that are limited to in-state resources are "facially discriminatory," or discriminate on their face (Elefant and Holt 2011). They must be justified by demonstrating that the state lacks alternatives to achieve legitimate policy goals (Elefant and Holt 2011). However, eligibility based on functional requirements such as interconnection, deliverability, or displacement of power, which can be functionally equivalent to in-state requirements, might not be viewed as discriminatory, and therefore, has lower risk of Commerce Clause challenges. States may be able to justify such policies because the size of requirements would place a minimal burden on commerce and offer legitimate benefits to the state, such as reliability and diversity of supplies that may not be readily achieved through other means (Elefant and Holt 2011).

2.4 Solar Alternative Compliance Payment Levels
Solar ACPs Generally Set a Ceiling on Prices and are Scheduled to Decline in Most Jurisdictions

The price of SRECs is generally limited by the solar ACP established by each state with a SREC market. If an entity obligated to meet the RPS cannot procure enough SRECs, it can pay the solar ACP for each megawatt-hour that it has not procured in the market. For this reason, the solar ACP essentially sets a ceiling on SREC prices, as obligated entities would not pay more than the level of the ACP to acquire SRECs for compliance. However, if SREC purchases are recoverable in rates and ACP payments are not, such as in Ohio and Missouri, it is possible that SREC payments could exceed the solar ACP. Payment of the ACP is generally the mechanism of last resort to achieve compliance with the RPS.

In most SREC jurisdictions, a solar ACP has been established either through legislation or by the state public utility commission (PUC). The solar ACP differs from the ACP established

---

[4] As of June 30, 2011, more than 940 MW of PV was installed or actively reserved through the California Solar Initiative program (CPUC 2011).

for RECs used to meet the main RPS resource targets. Solar ACPs are set at levels higher than main RPS ACPs to reflect the higher cost of solar energy and to enable adequate support for solar projects. In situations where obligated entities are having difficulties in meeting solar RPS targets, SREC prices rise to levels near the solar ACP, and in oversupply situations, the price of SRECs can fall well below the solar ACP.

Differences in solar ACP levels have affected SREC trading prices. For example, prices have been highest in New Jersey because New Jersey's solar ACP of nearly $700/MWh is significantly higher than solar ACPs in other states, which are in the $400–$500/MWh range. In Pennsylvania, solar ACPs are set at approximately twice the price paid for SRECs. In Missouri, there is a provision for non-compliance equal to twice the average market value of SRECs utilized for compliance during the period; non-compliance payments are not recoverable from ratepayers. North Carolina is unique in that there is no specific penalty or formula for assessing alternative compliance; it is up to the North Carolina PUC to enforce compliance. While Illinois has a significant solar carve out in its RPS, which takes effect in 2013, it is unclear if there will be a separate solar ACP (Wiser et al. 2010), which would be necessary to encourage a distinct SREC market. If there is not, SRECs would not trade above the price of the main RPS ACP.

Most states have established long-term schedules for solar ACPs that generally decline over time given the expectation that the price of solar will fall in coming years, consistent with recent trends (see Table 5). The availability of long-term solar ACP schedules helps provide some certainty to the market, enabling developers and financiers to price forward contracts. Solar ACPs decline over time in New Jersey, Ohio, and Maryland, and in Massachusetts, the state is authorized to reduce the rate but not by more than 10% in a compliance year (Table 5). Massachusetts recently decreased the solar ACP from $600/MWh to $550/MWh and proposed future levels for the next 10 years.

Table 5. State Solar Alternative Compliance Payments

State	Solar Alternative Compliance Payment
DC	$500/MWh through 2016, $350/MWh in 2017, $300/MWh in 2018, $200/MWh in 2019 and 2020, $150/MWh in 2021 and 2022, and $50/MWh in 2023 and thereafter
DE	$400/MWh for LSEs first year of use, $450/MWh in second year, $500/MWh in third and subsequent years
MA	$600/MWh in 2010; $550/MWh in 2011, 2012, and 2013; and proposed to decrease 5% each year through 2021
MD	$450/MWh for solar shortfalls in 2008, $400/MWh in 2009 through 2014, $350/MWh in 2015 and 2016, $200/MWh in 2017 and 2018, and continuing to decline by $50/MWh bi-annually until it reaches $50/MWh in 2023 and beyond
MO	Penalty of at least twice the average market value of SRECs for the calendar year
NC	No specified penalty but the North Carolina PUC is authorized to enforce compliance
NH	$163/MWh in 2011, adjusts annually based on Consumer Price Index
NJ	$693/MWh in EY 2010; declines by $16/MWh–$18/MWh annually through 2015
OH	$450/MWh in 2009, $400/MWh in 2010 and 2011; declines by $50/MWh every two years to meet a minimum of $50/MWh in 2024[a]
PA	Roughly twice the price paid for PV by electricity suppliers in the state[b]

[a] The Ohio PUC has the ability to increase the solar ACP if it determines entities are defaulting to the ACP rather than pursuing the necessary resources.
[b] The calculation also takes into account solar rebates, but this represents a small portion of the solar ACP.
Source: DSIRE 2011a

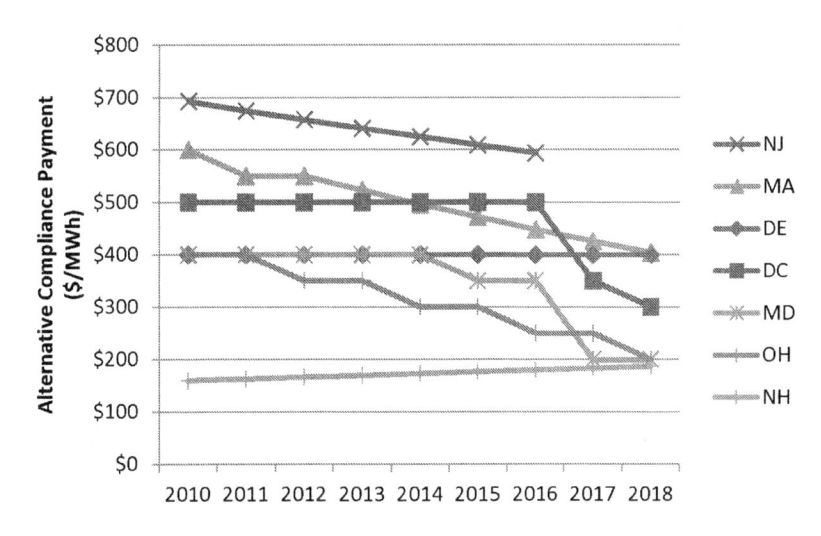

Figure 3. Solar alternative compliance payment levels over time

Source: DSIRE 2011a
Note: Massachusetts solar ACP levels for 2010 and 2011 are fixed; levels for 2012 and beyond have been proposed by the Department of Energy Resources but are not yet finalized.

2.5 Measurement and Verification Methods for SRECs
Methods of Verifying the Generation of SRECs Vary by System Size

Because SRECs can sell at high prices, an important issue is verifying the output from solar generators to ensure that the SRECs that are created match actual generation. Requirements for SREC measurement and verification vary to some degree across each state market. However, in general, most states allow small systems of less than about 10 kW to estimate annual generation based on models or engineering calculations. For example, models, such as PVWatts, are used to estimate the output of a facility based on system characteristics and average insolation for a particular location (Table 6). Typically for larger systems, a revenue grade meter is required to verify actual generation. This information is then self-reported to the REC tracking systems in most instances. Massachusetts has delegated the authority to independent monitors to report production data for participating SREC systems greater than 10 kW.

Table 6. State Requirements for Verifying Solar Output to Sell SRECs

State	Facility Reporting Provisions
DC	Facilities <10 kW can use estimated generation based on PVWatts calculation; otherwise, facilities can self-report via a revenue grade meter. Energy output of solar thermal systems >10,000 kWh per year must be rated and certified, and energy output must be determined by an onsite energy meter. Solar thermal systems ≤10,000 kWh per year may use an onsite energy meter or the annual performance measure determined by SRCC OG-300.
DE	Self-reporting via a revenue grade meter is used.
MA	All PV projects must self-report via a revenue grade meter to an independent verifier, the Massachusetts Clean Energy Technology Center. Projects <10 kW can report manually, while projects >10kW must report production using a data acquisition system (DAS). Currently there are 20 such DAS providers listed on the Massachusetts RPS website. The Massachusetts Clean Energy Technology Center maintains the production tracking system, verifies production data, and submits reports quarterly to NEPOOL-GIS.
MD	Facilities <10 kW may use estimated generation based on the PVWatts calculator. All other facilities must report monthly meter readings. Solar hot water systems must be certified and metered.
MO	Not yet determined.
NC	Projects installed "behind the meter" will be able to self-report their energy production data into the NC-RETS system to receive SRECs, while utility-metered projects will require a designated "Qualified Reporting Entity" with a separate NC-RETS account to upload generation data on their behalf. Systems >10 kW must be metered by the customer.
NH	All projects installed on the customer side of the meter, regardless of size, require an independent monitor for production verification.
NJ	Facilities <10 kW may use estimated generation based on the PVWatts calculator. All other facilities must report monthly meter readings.
OH	Self-reporting via revenue grade meter is used. If the system is ≤6 kW, generation can be reported from an inverter meter.
PA	Facilities >15 kW must report monthly meter readings. Facilities <15 kW are eligible to use estimated generation based on PVWatts calculation, unless they receive funding from the PA Sunshine Fund.

Sources: SRECTrade 2011a; Massachusetts DOER 2011a; Epsen 2011

States allowing solar thermal systems use a conversion factor to issue SRECs to solar thermal projects. Converting non-electric solar thermal output into a SREC equivalent is done using a conversion factor of 3,412,000 British thermal units (BTUs) to 1 SREC. This standard rate is used by states but only specified in implementation rules by North Carolina. In Washington, D.C., smaller systems use the kilowatt-hour (kWh) factor supplied by the Solar Rating and

Certification Corporation. Larger systems in Washington, D.C., must be metered; the BTU output is then converted to kilowatt-hours. Maryland specifies that BTUs created by solar thermal systems be converted to kilowatt-hours.

2.6 Long-Term Contracting and Financing Provisions
Lack of Long-Term Contracts Have Impeded Development in Some Cases: Some States Have Developed Mechanisms to Help Facilitate Financing

In some instances, reliance on spot market SREC prices has led to challenges in achieving compliance with solar carve outs, particularly in restructured electricity markets. Reliance on short-term spot markets for SRECs can pose problems for solar developers in obtaining the financing necessary to bring projects to fruition. Financiers (both debt and equity lenders) generally do not take SREC revenues into account unless a contract with a creditworthy purchaser is in place (Holt et al. 2011). This issue can be particularly problematic for large-scale systems that require debt or equity financing. At the same time, many electricity suppliers, especially in restructured electricity markets, resist signing contracts longer than two to three years. This may be because future loads, and therefore future solar compliance obligations, are unknown. Additionally, suppliers in regulated states may perceive some risk regarding cost recovery mechanisms if the contract extends beyond the current rate plan. As a result, some solar developers have had difficulty obtaining financing for their projects due to a lack of opportunities to enter long-term SREC contracts.

To address challenges in obtaining financing, some state policymakers have implemented provisions that reduce investor risk. As noted earlier, long-term solar ACP schedules can help reduce investor risk by providing knowledge of future price caps. In SREC markets, other provisions include: (1) requiring or encouraging long-term contracts or (2) establishing payment floors to set a minimum price for SRECs, which guarantee a minimum return. Also, some jurisdictions have implemented price responsive demand mechanisms through which future solar targets are reduced in the case of shortages or increased in the case of oversupplies. Also, many utilities in regulated electric markets offer long-term contracts for the SRECs and output of solar energy systems to facilitate development or elect to own solar projects.[5] In some jurisdictions, rebates or other types of incentives have been offered to reduce the risk and need to rely solely on SREC revenues, but we do not cover these programs in detail below.

Long-Term Contracting Requirements

State policymakers and regulators in New Jersey, Pennsylvania, and to a lesser extent Maryland encourage the use of long-term contracting to enable solar projects to obtain financing.

New Jersey has created a formal SREC-based financing program that awards long-term contracts through requests for proposals (RFPs) to help winning residential and commercial developers secure financing for their solar projects. The contracts resulting from the RFPs are standardized and non-negotiable, and developers are encouraged to bid SREC prices that

---

[5] Other mechanisms have been used to minimize or address investor risk, but these are generally outside the scope of SREC markets. Also, some states have used centralized procurement for their RPS.

would provide sufficient project returns. These programs represent only a fraction of the overall market, which called for about 320 MW$_{AC}$ of installed capacity in 2011 alone. The Jersey Central Power & Light, Atlantic City Energy, and Rockland Electric Company SREC-based financing programs were designed to support a total of 64 MW (name plate) from 2009 through 2011 (NERA Economic Consulting (2011b). The PSEG Solar Loan program had the goal of supporting 81 MW in the first two phases (NJ BPU 2011 d) (see Appendix for additional detail). As a result of these programs and perhaps other market conditions, long-term contracts have historically been more widely available in New Jersey than in other markets, making it easier for developers to operate and obtain financing. However, the availability of long-term contracts outside of the utility programs has declined recently with the drop-in SREC prices and signs of near-term oversupply in the market, as one might expect (SEIA/GTM 2011b; SEIA/GTM 2011c).

In Pennsylvania, the PUC issued a policy statement encouraging EDCs to conduct competitive solicitations for SRECs and procure SRECs from small-scale projects (<200 kW) through RFPs and bilateral contracts. It specifies that the price negotiated for SRECs from small-scale projects should not exceed the average winning bid price in the EDC's most recent RFPs for large-scale solar projects (Pennsylvania PUC 2011). In response, Pennsylvania EDCs have started to hold competitive solicitations to procure a portion of their SREC obligations over a longer delivery period (e.g., 7–10 years). The utilities are seeking bids in tranches (i.e., 100, 250, or 500 SRECs per year from an individual supplier). One of the utilities, PPL Electric Utilities, is issuing RFPs for individual projects as well as aggregations of projects <15 kW in size. These programs have not been large to date, however. The Met-Ed and Penelec solicitiations in 2010 were for 25,000 MWh while Penn Power and PPL Electric solicitations in 2011 were for a total of 46,000 MWh (see Table 10 and Appendix for additional details). The state is well ahead of its compliance targets, but this has been largely attributed to the availability of rebates that created an attractive incentive for projects (SEIA/GTM 2011b).

Maryland has a loose requirement aimed at helping buyers and sellers find each other and negotiate bilateral contracts. The Maryland Public Service Commission (PSC) requires solar generators to first offer their SRECs for sale on the PSC's website, if they want to sell directly to Maryland electricity suppliers requests for proposals. If the electricity suppliers enter into contracts directly with generators, the contracts must be for 15 years. Because long-term contracts are not required for purchases from brokers, most of the transactions in the market are broker-facilitated spot transactions (Mosier 2011). Therefore, this non-binding contracting requirement has had little effect in encouraging long-term contracts to date. Developers have indicated that the lack of long-term contracts makes it more difficult to secure financing for projects in Maryland because banks will not consider SREC revenues without a contract (SEIA/GTM 2011b). Therefore, developers have to take on more of this financial risk.

In Delaware, a long-term contracting program has been proposed. Delmarva Power applied to the Delaware PSC for the approval of a pilot SREC procurement program on September 16, 2011. Under the program, solar generators of different sizes could receive fixed SREC prices for 20 years. For example, small systems under 50 kW would receive $260/MWh for 10 years, followed by payments of $50/MWh for another 10 years. Larger systems of

250 kW to 2 MW would receive a bid price, if they submit winning bids. The program is slated to support a total of about 11,500 MWh, divided among four system size categories (Moore 2011).

Long-Term Price Floors

Long-term price floors have been implemented in Massachusetts and New Jersey by the distribution utility PSE&G (see Appendix for additional detail on these mechanisms). Theoretically, long-term price floors serve the same purpose as long-term contracts. If a long-term price floor is structured in a way that guarantees a minimum value for SRECs in future years, investors may view it as they would a binding SREC contract.

In Massachusetts, the Solar Credit Clearinghouse was established in 2010 with the goal of establishing a minimum price to encourage development. The program enables any unsold SRECs in a compliance period to be auctioned at a minimum price of approximately $300/MWh. The useful life of SRECs is extended once they are submitted into an auction account, and the lifetime can be extended further if the SRECs do not sell at auction initially. So far, the program is untested because no auctions have been held due to shortages in the market. Despite its complexity and initial reservations about the program, investors are becoming more comfortable with this market design (SEIA/GTM 2011b). However, the program structure does not guarantee the sale of SRECs if the final auction does not clear. Also, it does not guarantee cash flows in a particular year. For example, if a SREC is not cleared during an auction and its shelf-life is extended and it is sold in a later year, the inability to receive payments in the first year can impact the return on a project.

In New Jersey, the PSE&G loan program has an element of a price floor to provide confidence to consumers regarding the repayment of the loan. Under the program, PSE&G offers loans that cover 40%–60% of the cost of a PV system. Customers may repay the loan principal and interest through cash payments or by signing their SRECs over to PSE&G. Throughout the 15-year loan term, PSE&G credits customers for each SREC generated based on market prices but not below the established price floor, which is initially $420/MWh for residential systems. While spot prices have historically been much higher than these levels, this situation may be changing. Forward prices for 2012 recently fell well below the $420/MWh price floor, which may mean that the utility will have to recover the price differential from ratepayers. However, this remains to be seen.

Price Responsive Demand

The Massachusetts program also incorporates mechanisms to adjust the solar targets based on compliance with targets. These provisions can help regulate the supply and demand balance and reduce risks of an oversupplied market. For example, under the Massachusetts Solar Credit Clearinghouse program, the term that SRECs can be deposited in the auction is adjusted based on market conditions. Initially projects can opt to deposit SRECs in the auction account for up to 10 years of the life of the system, but that can be reduced if the market is oversupplied. Additionally, the compliance targets in Massachusetts are increased by the amount of SRECs deposited in the auction in a given compliance year to temper situations of oversupply (see Appendix for additional details).

Utility Standard Offer or Long-Term Contracts

In traditionally regulated or hybrid electricity markets, such as North Carolina, Missouri, and Ohio, utilities offer fixed long-term contracts to solar generators to facilitate in-state solar development. Standard offer contracts can help the economics of small to mid-sized projects in particular. They provide certainty regarding the price that consumers can obtain for their SRECs, although they may not significantly influence the ability of retail customers to obtain loans for their projects. In general, payment terms have ranged from $30/MWh to $300/MWh for terms ranging from 5 to 20 years. Most of these programs have been offered on a trial basis, with limits on the enrollment period (one or two years) or limits on the overall capacity that can participate in the program (see text box for examples).

Overall, the New Jersey long-term contracting provisions have been effective in driving new renewable energy development and enabling projects to obtain financing. However, falling SREC prices may mean that ratepayers will need to pay the difference between the long-term contracts offered by the distribution utilities and market prices. The price floor mechanism in Massachusetts has yet to be fully tested as the auction mechanism has not yet been used, but developers and investors may be gaining comfort with this model, according to industry analysts (SEIA/GTM 2011b). Fixed long-term contracts will continue to be important to drive in-state solar energy development in other markets; however, as many of the existing programs have limited funds or are available for a limited duration, it is unclear if they will be extended in future years.

Sample Utility Long-Term SREC Purchasing Programs to Encourage Small to Mid-Sized Systems

As a method of procuring SRECs, several utilities in Missouri, North Carolina, and Ohio have developed SREC long-term purchasing programs for retail customers. These programs are either structured as standard offer contracts for SRECs, or upfront incentives, which are awarded in exchange for the right to keep the SRECs for a pre-defined number of years.

Ameren Missouri was the first utility to develop a standard offer contract program for solar in Missouri. Customers installing systems with a nameplate capacity of less than 10 kW may sell SRECs for $100/MWh on a 10-year upfront basis, based on PVWatts estimates of output. Systems between 10 kW up to 100 kW in size may sell SRECs for $100/MWh on a 5-year basis based on actual generation from their metered output (Ameren 2011b). The program, which is separate from the solar rebate required by law, was funded with $2 million for 2011, and all funding was committed as of mid-May 2011 with contracts completed or pending for 2,269 SRECs (Ameren 2011a). Ameren may continue the program in 2012 and 2013, but it has not been submitted to the PUC (Ameren 2011a; Ameren 2011b).

Duke Energy Carolinas launched a standard offer purchase program for RECs including SRECs in North Carolina in 2008. Under the program, the utility enters into contracts ranging from 5 years to a maximum term of 15 years. Contracts must be for at least 35 MWh/year of SRECs (approximately the output of a 25-kW system). Solar systems that generate more than 250 MWh/year are ineligible and can submit an unsolicited bid proposal to the utility instead. In 2010, customers were paid $30/MWh for SRECs under the standard offer program (this represents the price for the SRECs only, not the underlying electricity). SREC prices escalate annually for each standing contract. Prices will ultimately increase to $42/MWh in 2025 (Duke Energy Carolinas 2011).

In Ohio, **Duke Energy Ohio** offers a residential PV REC purchase program that was approved in July 2010. The program is available through December 31, 2012, to Duke's residential customers, including both customers purchasing their electric generation service from Duke and those purchasing from other retail suppliers. The REC purchase agreements have a term of 15 years. Customers received $300/MWh for SRECs procured in 2010, and payment levels will be adjusted in subsequent years based on market prices (Duke Energy Ohio 2011a).

Progress Energy Carolinas (Progress) has a similar standard purchase offer for North and South Carolina non-residential customers called the SunSense Commercial PV Program. Progress pays $180/MWh for both the electricity and SRECs generated by the PV system for a period of at least 20 years. To be eligible, the PV systems must have a nameplate capacity between 11 kW_{DC} and 500 kW_{DC}. Annual program participation is limited to 5 MW and net metering is not offered. Systems owned and operated by a third-party on a Progress Energy customer's property are also eligible. For residential systems sized 2 kW_{AC} to 10 kW_{AC} the utility provides a $1/watt$_{AC}$ upfront incentive and a monthly bill credit based on the AC rating of $4.5/kW (Progress Energy Carolinas 2011b).

First Energy ran a residential REC purchasing program in Ohio in the service territories of Ohio Edison, The Illuminating Company, and Toledo Edison's between 2009 and May 31, 2011. Under the program, First Energy offered 15-year contracts for residential SRECs. The price paid was determined through a biannual RFP process. The PUCO and FirstEnergy determined that if the utility was unable to procure SRECs through competitive solicitations, an alternative purchase price would be offered to residential customers. The price offered for SRECs from residential systems was $360/MWh in 2009 and $320/MWh in 2010 and 2011, decreasing by $40/MWh every two years over the lifetime of the contract (DSIRE 2011c).

AEP Ohio began offering an incentive program for both residential and non-residential customers called the Renewable Energy Technology Program Rider in July 2011. The two-year program is funded at $1 million annually for solar. The current solar incentive is $1.50 per Watt, and this payment is provided to customers in exchange for the SRECs generated by the project for a 15-year period (AEP Ohio 2011).

2.7 Rate Caps
Rate Caps Have Yet to be Reached Although Policy Implementation is in Early Stages

Going forward, the need for obligated entities to meet solar carve outs can be influenced by the presence of electricity rate impact caps. These caps were established by legislators to limit the ratepayer impacts of RPS policies or, in some cases, the solar carve out in particular.

Rate caps exist in some form in five SREC markets (Maryland, Delaware, Ohio, Missouri, and North Carolina) but have not been reached or are yet to be evaluated (Table 7). Delaware and Maryland have rate caps on the cost of the solar set-aside requirement, while other states have caps on the entire RPS.

In Delaware, the cost of compliance includes costs associated with any ratepayer-funded rebate program, SREC purchases, and solar ACPs. If these costs exceed 1% of the total retail cost of electricity, then the PSC may freeze the solar requirement; Delaware also has a 3% cap on its RPS (14 DE Reg 1241, 3.2.16). This provision went into effect in July 2010, so the impact cannot be assessed until after utility compliance reports are filed in September 2011 (Stewart 2011).

Table 7. Rate Cap on RPS or Solar Set-Aside

Rate Cap on RPS	Rate Cap on Solar Set-Aside	No Rate Cap
OH: 3% increase in generation costs	**DE:** 1% increase in retail rates (combination of solar set-aside, rebates, and solar ACPs together)*	
NC: Caps on annual cost per account for incremental RPS costs; varies by customer class and year	**MD:** 1% increase in retail rates (solar set-aside only); allows for 1-year delay in meeting solar RPS	DC, PA, MA, NH, NJ**
MO: 1% increase in retail rates		

Source: Wiser et al. 2010; DSIRE 2011a; N.J.A.C 14:8-2.2 and 2.3, revised effective March 30, 2011.
* Delaware also has a 3% cap on its RPS.
**New Jersey previously had a rate cap of 2%, but the provision was removed as of March 2011.

In Maryland, the increase is based on the actual or projected dollar-for-dollar cost to purchase SRECs. If that cost is 1% or more of a supplier's total annual electricity sales revenues, then compliance can be delayed by one year (DSIRE 2011a). No requests have yet been made to delay compliance in Maryland (PSC MD 2011).

Ohio, Missouri, and North Carolina have rate caps on the entire RPS policy. In Ohio, the increase is based on "reasonably expected" rate increases of no more than 3%. If rates are expected to increase by 3% or more above what they would have otherwise been, the cap goes into effect (DSIRE 2011a).

In Missouri, utilities may be excused from their obligation if the cost of complying with the RPS increases retail electricity rates by more than 1% in any year. If this occurs, the requirement will be adjusted in that year so that the rate cap is not violated (DSIRE 2011a). In their RPS planning dockets, no utilities in Missouri indicated potential shortages in SREC supply, likely due to the fact that they can obtain SRECs from out-of-state markets. One utility, Ameren, noted that it was able to procure SRECs at an average price of about $8/MWh. Ameren's total projected compliance cost in 2011 was $5.3 million, which represents 0.01% of Ameren's total revenue requirement (Ameren 2011b). Similarly, Kansas City Power & Light and KCP&L Greater Missouri Operations Company estimated that the average increase in annual revenue requirement would be 0.14% on a 3-year average and 0.04% on a 10-year average (KCP&L-GMO 2011), which is far less than the 1% rate cap.

North Carolina's RPS legislation takes a different approach to capping costs. Utilities can recover up to a maximum dollar amount of "incremental costs" annually from each customer class (residential, commercial, and industrial). In 2011, for example, utilities were allowed to recover a maximum of $10 per residential account, $50 per commercial account, and $500 per industrial account (N.C. Gen. Stat. § 62-133.8(h)(4)).

In the future, it is possible that rate caps may be reached; whether they will be reached will depend on many factors, including future SREC costs and overall retail rates. Generally, the likelihood of reaching a cap is greater in states that cap the impact of the solar carve out (as opposed to the entire RPS) and also have aggressive solar targets.

3 SREC Market Trends

3.1 Trading Volumes and Market Activity
Most SRECs Have Been Sourced from New Jersey; Other Markets Are Expanding

In recent years, the vast majority of SREC trading has occurred in New Jersey. Data on the source of SRECs traded or retired to meet state solar carve outs are available from the REC tracking systems used by the states to track RPS compliance.[6] Trading and retirement data are generally similar for these markets, but SRECs could be traded multiple times before they are retired for compliance with a state solar carve out.

Figure 4 shows SRECs issued in 2010 in the PJM Interconnection balancing area, the most active region for SREC trading. PJM data provide a good indication of total SREC activity because most states with SREC policies are in or can sell into the PJM balancing authority, with notable exceptions being Massachusetts, New Hampshire, and to some extent North Carolina.[7] In 2010, 75% of the SRECs issued in PJM were located in New Jersey, followed by Pennsylvania (11%), Ohio (6%), and Maryland (4%). Other states include SRECs from projects located in Virginia, North Carolina, Washington, D.C., and West Virginia. Data through October 2011 show similar general trends, with Pennsylvania seeing a higher percentage of issued SRECs (17%).

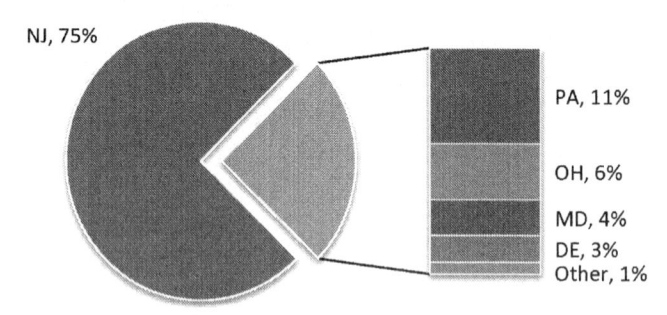

Figure 4. SRECs issued in PJM-GATS, 2010

Source: PJM-GATS 2011a

Solar capacity additions in recent years are consistent with the SREC trading data (see Table 8 and Figure 4). Of the states with SREC markets in 2010, New Jersey led installed PV by far, with 260 MW of cumulatively installed PV capacity, much of which came online in

---

[6] PJM-Generation Attribute System (PJM-GATS), the REC tracking system for the PJM balancing authority, provides information about the source of SRECs retired for each solar set-aside in the region. The majority of states with SREC markets are in PJM. This information is available on the Public Reports page of the PJM-GATS website, under the heading "RPS Retired Certificates (Reporting Year)" (PJM-GATS 2011a). Massachusetts, Missouri, New Hampshire, and North Carolina employ different systems to track RPS compliance. Missouri uses the North American Renewables Registry (NARR), Massachusetts and New Hampshire use the NEPOOL Generation Information System (GIS) in New England, and North Carolina uses the NC-Renewable Energy Tracking System (NCRETS), which currently accepts credit transfers from the Midwest Renewable Energy Tracking System (M-RETS), NARR, the Western Renewable Energy Generation Information System (WREGIS), and the Electric Reliability Council of Texas (ERCOT) REC tracking system.
[7] PV systems in North Carolina must choose whether to register in NC-RETS or the PJM-GATS system.

2010, followed by Pennsylvania, North Carolina, and Massachusetts (Sherwood 2011). Note that North Carolina and Massachusetts are not included in the PJM-GATS SREC trading volume data. Missouri installations totaled less than 1 MW, but the Missouri solar requirement does not take effect until 2011.

Table 8. PV Capacity Additions (Annual and Cumulative)

State	2009 PV Additions MW$_{DC}$	2010 PV Additions MW$_{DC}$	Cumulative Installed Capacity MW$_{DC}$
DC	0.3	3.5	4.5
DE	1.4	2.4	5.6
MA	9.6	20.4	38.2
MD	4.7	3.4	10.9
MO	0.1	0.5	0.7
NC	6.6	28.7	40.0
NH	0.5	1.3	2.0
NJ	57.3	132.4	259.9
OH	0.6	18.7	20.7
PA	4.4	46.5	54.8

Source: Sherwood 2011
Notes: Figures here are calendar year additions. Capacity for each state represents in-state generation, although some states allow out-of-state capacity to contribute.

The dominance of SREC trades from New Jersey systems is not surprising because the New Jersey solar requirement was the first to take effect, its solar carve out is currently more than four times larger than the next largest state's requirement, and its interconnection requirements are such that only in-state resources can meet its standard. Further, New Jersey has had the highest SREC prices in the region. However, there has been a move toward greater geographic diversity of SREC markets. Monthly SREC trading data in PJM show an uptick in volumes traded in markets other than New Jersey in 2010 and 2011 (see Figure 5), particularly from systems in Maryland, Pennsylvania, and Ohio.

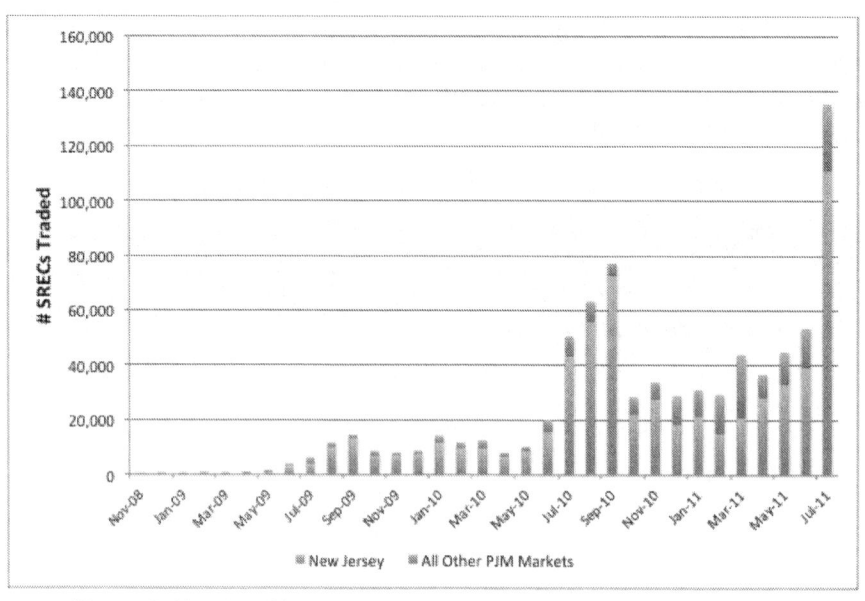

Figure 5. Monthly SREC trading volumes in PJM-GATS, 2009–2011

SRECs can also be sold into voluntary markets in which individuals, businesses, and institutions make voluntary purchases of RECs to match their own electricity consumption. However, voluntary SREC transactions have been limited to date. In 2010, SRECs represented 0.2% of U.S. voluntary market sales, which includes sales by utility green pricing programs, competitive green power programs, and unbundled REC purchases (Heeter and Bird 2011). In some instances utilities use SRECs to include solar in the resource mix of utility green power programs offered to residential and small commercial customers, but they are a relatively small fraction of total program supplies. In 2010, utility programs procured about 39,000 MWh of solar energy to supply 0.8% of the green energy sold through their green pricing programs (Heeter and Bird 2011). In some instances, utilities have offered fixed-price, long-term contracts for the solar energy output and used the SRECs to supply green pricing programs. For example, the Tennessee Valley Authority (TVA) and North Carolina Green Power purchase the SRECs from PV system owners for a fixed fee of $0.10–$0.12/kWh for an established period such as 10 years and supply their green power programs with the SRECs (TVA 2011; NCGP 2011).

3.2 In-State Versus Out-of-State Sourcing
Several States are Sourcing SRECs Primarily from In-State Systems, While Others are Sourcing More Broadly

The location of solar projects providing SRECs is also highly dependent on rules regarding whether states can source SRECs from in-state or out-of-state facilities, as mentioned earlier. As a result of policies that allow regional sourcing, some developers are registering their projects in multiple states, particularly within the PJM balancing authority, to increase their opportunities to sell SRECs. However, the majority of systems are being used for compliance in state. Of the roughly 17,000 PV facilities registered in PJM-GATS,[8] 83% are registered for use in the SREC market of just one state, 12% are registered in two states, 5% are registered in three states, and 0.9% are registered in four states (PJM-GATS 2011b). Table 9 shows the number and aggregate capacity of PV systems registered for use in PJM-GATS states, as well as Massachusetts and North Carolina.[9]

Table 9. In-State Versus Out-of-State Project Registration as of October 2011

State	Registration	Number of Projects	Capacity (MW$_{DC}$)
DC	In State	371	2.2
	Potential Imports	1,961	18.1
	Potential Exports	137	0.8
DE	In State	889	22.7
	Potential Imports	0	0.0
	Potential Exports	655	7.4
MA	In State	1,015	41.1
	Potential Imports	N/A	N/A
	Potential Exports	N/A	N/A
MD	In State	1,748	30.9
	Potential Imports	778	21.2
	Potential Exports	251	11.8
NJ	In State	10,170	417.0
	Potential Imports	N/A	N/A
	Potential Exports	35	5.7
NC	In State	125	63.3
	Potential Imports	80	41.2
	Potential Exports	75	1.7
OH	In State	417	27.5
	Potential Imports	2,752	57.9
	Potential Exports	144	1.3
PA	In State	4,873	110.7
	Potential Imports	1,503	37.7
	Potential Exports	2,683	58.6

Sources: PJM-GATS 2011b; Massachusetts DOER 2011b
Note: "In state" refers to projects located within a particular state and registered only in that state. "Potential imports" refers to projects located in other states that are registered for potential use in the specified state. "Potential exports" refers to projects in the specified state that are registered for potential use to meet compliance obligations in other states. The majority of these potential export facilities are also registered in the state where they are located. As of August 1, 2011, the potential imports to Washington, D.C., decreased as a result of the District's decision to limit out-of-state generation.

---

[8] Typically projects are certified by state agencies for compliance and then registered in PJM-GATS. Registered generators are all generating units that have an account with the GATS administrator. The facilities in the GATS database are operational.
[9] No PV systems are registered yet in Missouri's chosen tracking system, NARR. The first compliance year in Missouri is 2011.

Two states—New Jersey and Massachusetts—source all of their SRECs from in-state resources as required by state law. In another approach, Maryland regulations required electricity suppliers to seek SRECs first from generators on the Maryland distribution grid, meaning that suppliers could only procure SRECs from out of state if there were no available in-state resources. In 2010, Maryland electricity suppliers sourced 63% of the total SRECs retired from in-state generators, with about another quarter from Illinois, a state without a SREC market or solar carve out (see Figure 6a). In 2012, a binding in-state requirement goes into effect in Maryland (DSIRE 2011b).

In other markets, the source of SRECs retired for compliance requirements is more diverse. Washington, D.C.-based solar generators only provided 13% of SRECs retired to meet the D.C. standard in 2010. SRECs used for compliance in Washington, D.C., have come from 14 other states, including a number of states without SREC markets or solar carve outs, such as Virginia (see Figure 6b). In Washington, D.C., external facilities are five times more numerous than facilities located within the District (see Table 9). Although Washington, D.C.'s previous law stated a preference for in-district resources, its newly adopted law (August 2011) has a more stringent local requirement, starting in 2011. Out-of-state projects certified for the RPS program by January 31, 2011, will be eligible to continue to sell into the Washington, D.C., market.

While Pennsylvania has a substantial amount of registered in-state facilities, only about one-third of SRECs supplying Pennsylvania's solar requirement were sourced from in-state facilities in 2010. The remainder was sourced from six other states, with the largest contributors being Delaware (41%) and Illinois (25%) (see Figure 7a). A small fraction of SRECs have been retired from systems located in a variety of states within PJM to meet the Pennsylvania solar standard (see Figure 7a). Pennsylvania systems are also being retired for compliance with requirements in Washington, D.C., and Ohio.

Despite the 50% in-state requirement in Ohio, only 35% of SRECs retired in 2010 were sourced from Ohio (see Figure 7b). This may be the case because Ohio utilities and competitive providers did not achieve full compliance with the unadjusted solar carve outs in 2010; several entities successfully petitioned to have their 2010 targets adjusted downward, with any shortfall to be made up in 2011 (Siegfried 2011). In Ohio, there are about six times as many out-of-state facilities registered (see Table 9). Pennsylvania contributed 63% of the total SRECs retired to date for compliance with the Ohio solar target.

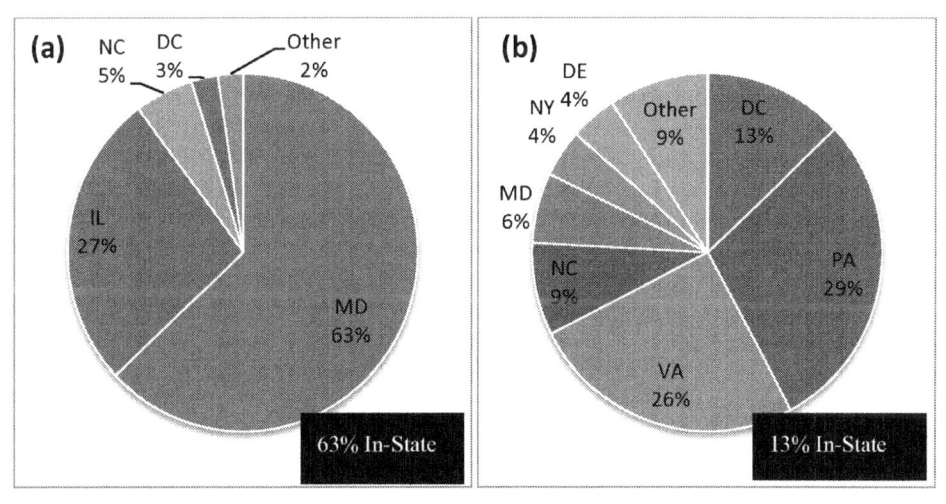

Figure 6. (a) Source of SRECs retired for 2010 compliance in Maryland (b) Source of SRECs retired for 2010 compliance in Washington, D.C.

Source: PJM-GATS 2011a
(a) Other includes: DE, IN, NY, OH, PA, VA, WV
(b) Other includes: IL, IN, KY, MI, NJ, OH, WI, WV

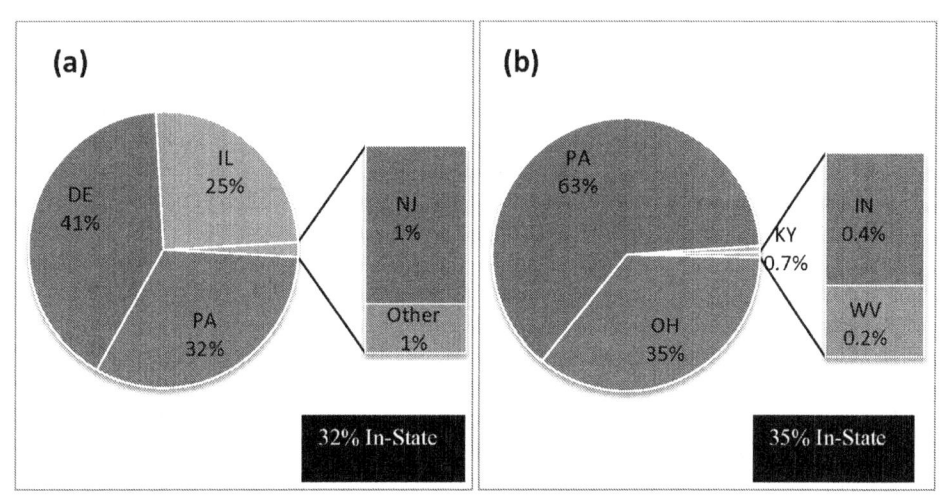

Figure 7. (a) Source of SRECs retired for 2010 compliance in Pennsylvania (b) Source of SRECs retired for 2010 compliance in Ohio

Source: PJM-GATS 2011a
(a) Other includes: MD, VA, WV

In North Carolina, the utilities are sourcing SRECs from both out-of-state projects, which are limited to 25% of the standard, as well as from in-state sources. Duke Energy Carolinas maintains a diverse solar portfolio, including: Duke-owned PV installations (at its central sites and at distributed sites[10]), credits purchased from out-of-state suppliers (which can be used for up to 25% of compliance requirements), credits purchased from in-state PV and

---

[10] Under the Duke Energy PV DG Program, Duke has secured 25 sites and installed roughly 9.9 MW$_{DC}$ (estimated to generate 13,485 MWh annually) (Duke Energy 2011c).

solar thermal projects, and credits purchased from a standard offer contract program available to the residential and commercial sectors (Duke Energy 2011b). Similarly, Progress Energy Carolinas purchases SRECs from in-state and out-of-state generators, as well as through the utility's standard offer contract program (Progress Energy Carolinas 2011a).

In Missouri, the three investor-owned utilities (IOUs) plan to procure most of their SRECs from solar projects in the West that were registered in WREGIS, according to plans filed in 2011 (Ameren 2011b; KCP&L 2011; KCP&L-GMO 2011). Additionally, Ameren plans to source some SRECs both from a 100 kW installation on their company headquarters and some through entering into standard offer contracts with residential and commercial customers (Ameren 2011b). For the 2011–2013 planning period, Ameren Missouri plans to procure SRECs from out-of-state sources, through a continuation of their standard offer program, potentially through utility-scale installations at several of its existing generating facilities and through unsolicited proposals from solar developers (Ameren 2011b). The other two utilities plan to continue to meet the solar requirement by purchasing SRECs from out-of-state projects through brokers due to price considerations and uncertainty regarding the solar carve out and RPS (KCP&L 2011; KCP&L-GMO 2011).

3.3 Size of Systems Supplying SRECs
SREC Markets are Supporting a Mix of PV System Sizes; Large Systems are Increasingly Common

Policymakers may be interested in ensuring that SREC markets support a mix of system sizes in order to: (1) increase the supply of decentralized, local power generation at customer sites; (2) establish support for a variety of contractors, installers, and developers; and/or (3) ensure that a variety of customer types benefit from ratepayer-funded programs. These goals may also be balanced with an interest in achieving solar targets at least cost.

To date, most markets are supporting a mix of residential and mid- to large-sized commercial PV systems, but large systems are increasingly dominating capacity in some markets (see Figure 8). In all markets except North Carolina, approximately two-thirds or more of the total number of registered projects are smaller than 10 kW (see Figure 8), with mid-sized (10 kW to 250 kW) projects generally contributing substantially to the total project number. In North Carolina, about 15% of registered projects are smaller than 10 kW, nearly 50% are mid-sized, and the remainder is large projects that are greater than 250 kW in size.

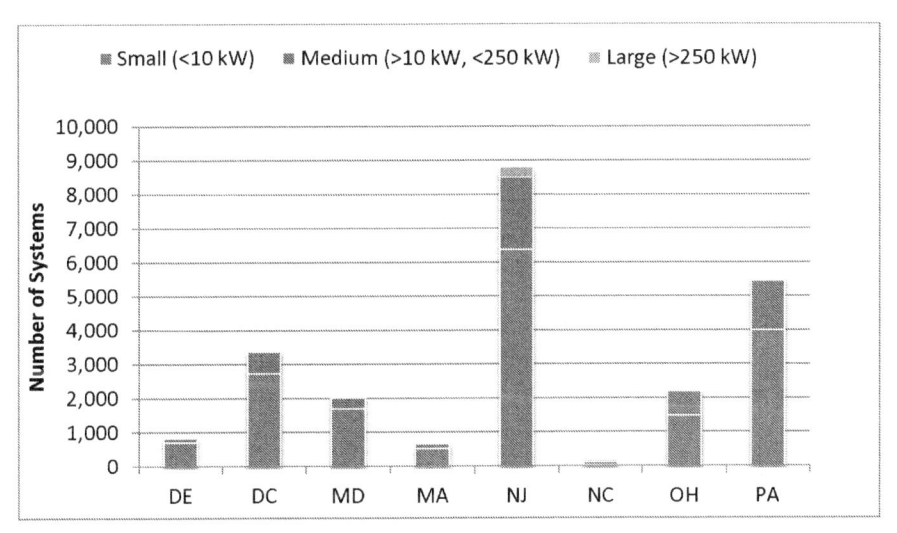

Figure 8. Number of PV projects by size and jurisdiction

Sources: Project registration data. PJM-GATS 2011b; Massachusetts DOER 2011b; N.C. Utility Commission 2011a

Figure 9 shows the relative contribution of small (<10 kW), mid-sized (10 kW to <250 kW), and large systems (>250 kW) to total registered solar capacity. Large projects currently dominate registered capacity in a few markets—most notably, North Carolina, Massachusetts, and New Jersey. For example, although nearly 75% of the 8,800 projects in New Jersey are smaller than 10 kW, they represent 12% of the aggregate capacity. In North Carolina, projects greater than 250 kW represent more than 90% of the aggregate capacity, while small projects account for less than 1%.

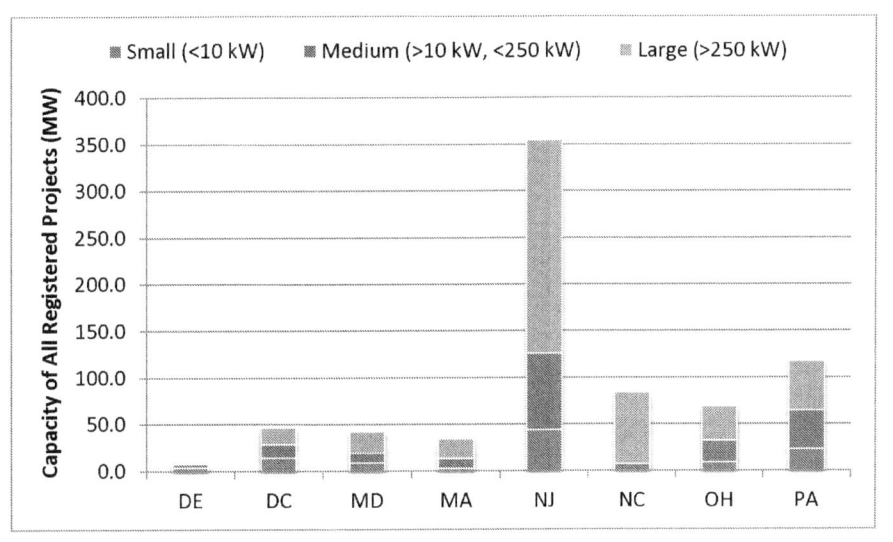

Figure 9. Aggregate capacity (in MW) of registered PV projects by size and jurisdiction

Sources: PJM-GATS 2011b; Massachusetts DOER 2011b; NCUC 2011a

Small residential and commercial systems may inherently face additional barriers in SREC markets. Small systems may not be as economic as larger systems due to the lack of efficiencies of scale, although this may be offset by the fact that residential systems displace higher retail electricity rates. Consumers may have a difficult time finding buyers for their SRECs; buyers are often interested in purchasing large quantities at once to minimize transaction costs. In addition, small consumers may not be able to access complex incentive programs, where they are required to bid into a competitive process. Lastly, small system owners may not want to take on the risk of uncertain future SREC revenues.

Available data suggest that these challenges have not prohibited the development of small systems in most states to date, however. In most markets, SREC aggregators are helping small residential and small commercial projects sell their SRECs. For example, in Massachusetts, 99.8% of small-sized projects and 91% of mid-sized projects were part of an aggregation, as of July 2011 (Massachusetts DOER 2011b). In the rest of PJM, 55% of small systems and 40% of mid-sized projects participate in aggregations (Bowery 2011). Often utilities have used standard offers, auctions, and solicitations to help encourage development of projects in various size categories. Under these programs, utilities purchase the SRECs under long-term contracts, which provide a stable incentive for system owners. In Missouri, North Carolina, and Ohio, regulated utilities have created standard offer programs for their retail customers who are interested in installing behind-the-meter systems on their homes or businesses (see text box in Section 2.6).

Additionally, separate from standard offer programs, other LSEs have solicited long-term SREC contracts from developers of both small and large projects through competitive solicitations and auctions. Since most LSEs in an unregulated market do not want to sign a contract beyond the scope of their demand requirement, competitive solicitation and auction programs have been an important way for independent power producers to obtain long-term contracts. The New Jersey SREC-Based Financing Program (see Appendix) solicits SRECs from projects up to 2 MW_{DC} in size. The program has a small project size segment (<50 kW) and a large project size segment (50–2,000 kW). Also, Pennsylvania utility PPL Electric Utilities has chosen to procure SRECs from projects <10 kW through a "Small Scale Solar Set-Aside" RFP targeted at SREC aggregators (Appendix). These programs have been important for encouraging a mix of system sizes in these states.

System size has been trending larger in recent years. There has been a steady increase in the number of PV projects larger than 250 kW. The number of systems greater than 250 kW has grown cumulatively from just two in 2003 to nearly 400 through the first half of 2011. Since 2008, the average size of projects in this class has been greater than 600 kW. As expected, the average has been skewed by the installation of some large utility-scale projects in recent years. For example, as shown in Figure 10, the average size of this class of projects was 1.1 MW in 2009, which is much higher than previous years due to the completion of several utility-scale projects.

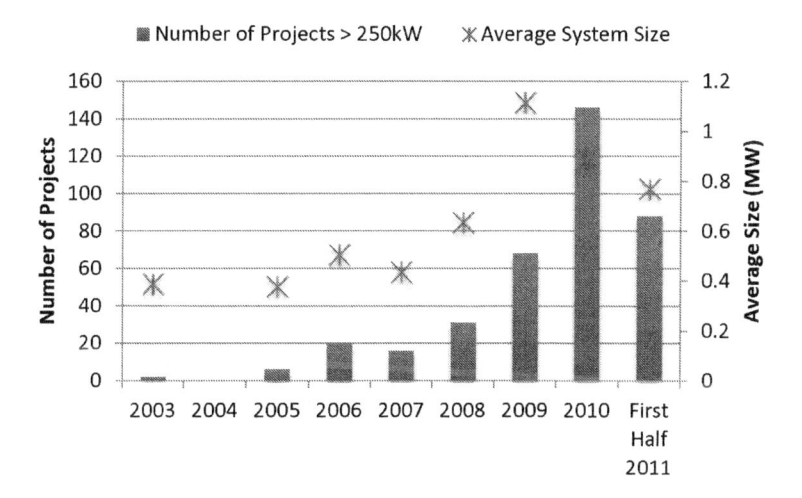

Figure 10. Number and average size of facilities >250 kW installed annually in PJM-GATS
Source: PJM-GATS 2011b

Utility-scale PV projects >1 MW have played an increasingly larger role in the markets in recent years. New Jersey leads in utility-scale solar deployment with 51 solar projects >1 MW operational as of August 2011 (PJM-GATS 2011b). North Carolina currently has 22 in-state generators >1 MW completed (NCUC 2011a). Massachusetts has three operational PV generators >1 MW (Massachusetts DOER 2011b), and Delaware is home to a 10 MW solar park commissioned this year (SEIA 2011).

A number of large projects are planned over the next few years. In aggregate, these planned projects could result an estimated 400 MW of new PV deployment. There is variation in estimates of planned capacity and some projects may not come to fruition, but these data are indicative. Figure 11 shows the aggregate capacity of PV projects completed versus planned as of September 2011.

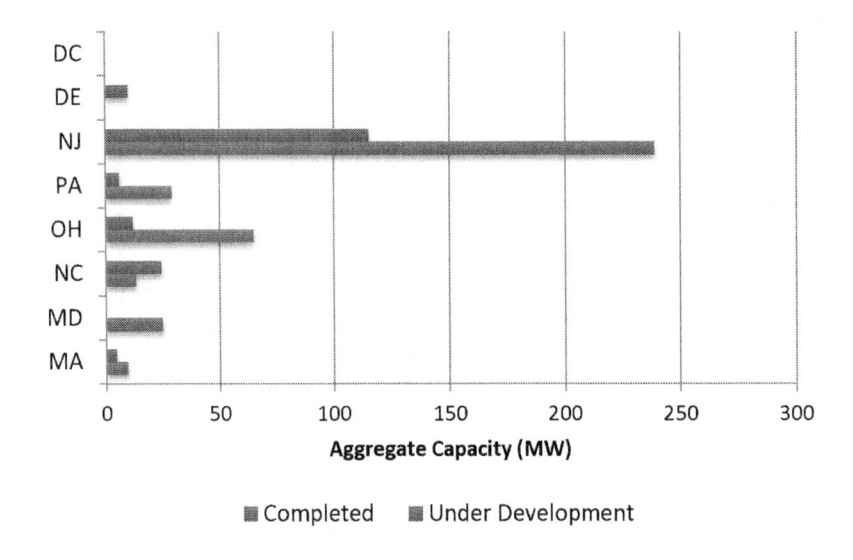

Figure 11. Aggregate capacity of utility scale (>1 MW) PV projects (completed and under development)

Sources: PJM-GATS 2011a; Massachusetts DOER 2011b; NCUC 2011a; SEIA 2011; SEPA 2011; NJ BPU 2011c
Note: The New Jersey estimate for projects under development is derived from the list of projects that have registered with the NJ BPU under the SRP program prior to construction but have not yet been completed.

Large projects can help states achieve compliance more quickly. However, they may flood the market with excess credits, which could reduce SREC prices, potentially to levels that could no longer provide adequate incentives for small PV systems. In Ohio, two utility-scale PV facilities are planned for the near term. Together, if completed, the 12-MW Wyandot Solar Facility and the 50-MW Turning Point facility would produce an estimated 24% of the total Ohio SREC requirement in 2013, according to an estimate by SRECTrade (SRECTrade 2011b).

Two main mechanisms are used by states to limit the impact of large systems on the market. The first mechanism is to place a cap on the size of systems eligible to sell SRECs—2 of the 10 jurisdictions currently have such a cap. In Massachusetts, solar generators must be smaller than 6 MW_{DC} in order to generate SRECs. Washington, D.C., adopted legislation effective August 1, 2011, which caps systems eligible to generate SRECs at 5 MW. Pennsylvania has considered capping system size. Before 2010, New Jersey had a 2-MW DC cap, which was lifted to help keep pace with aggressive solar growth targets.[11] The other mechanism is to establish separate standards for customer-sited and large-scale systems. For example, Colorado (which does not have a tradable SREC market) requires half of the solar carve out to come from customer-sited systems (DSIRE 2011a).

---

[11] New Jersey has no specific limits, but systems must be connected to the distribution grid, and behind-the-meter projects must be sized so that annual output does not exceed annual on-site load (DSIRE 2011d).

3.4 SREC Prices

New Jersey has Historically Experienced the Highest Prices; Recent or Forward Prices Have Dropped Significantly in Most Markets

SREC prices tend to track the supply and demand in the state or regional market. Spot pricing for SRECs is publically available from platforms like SRECTrade and FlettExchange.[12] SRECTrade hosts a monthly auction, while Flett Exchange is an online exchange. Both platforms cover markets in PJM states, Massachusetts, and Ohio, and similar price trends can be seen in reported data from both companies. Figure 12 shows SREC prices for the current or nearest compliance year.

Historically, SRECs from New Jersey have seen the highest prices, ranging from $400/MWh to approximately $650/MWh in recent years, while SRECs from most other states have ranged from $200/MWh to $500/MWh (Figure 12). However, in 2011, SREC prices fell, sometimes dramatically, in all markets except for in-state Massachusetts and Ohio. In New Jersey, spot prices fell from between $600/MWh and $700/MWh in 2009 and 2010 to less than $200/MWh in September 2011 (Figure 12).

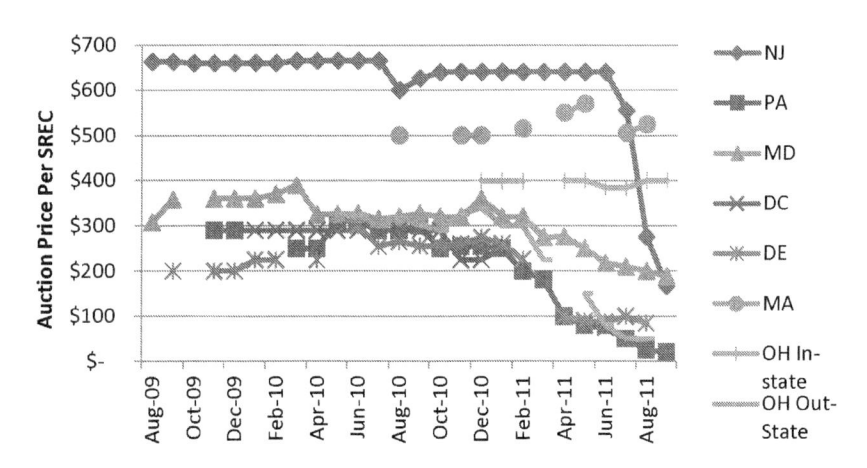

Figure 12. SREC spot prices (per MWh), August 2009 to September 2011
Source: SRECTrade 2011c

Long-term contract prices can differ substantially from spot prices. Solicitations held by EDCs in New Jersey for procuring SRECs in 10- or 15-year contracts have resulted in SREC prices lower than spot prices in 2009 and 2010. In February 2011 and June 2011, average

---

[12] PJM-GATS reports solar weighted average prices for transactions in the PJM market (see PJM-GATS 2011c) that differ from spot prices reported by SRECTrade and Flett Exchange because PJM-GATS pricing can include pricing from long- or mid-term contracts as well as spot prices. PJM-GATS reports prices on a monthly basis, based on when the SREC was issued, traded, or retired, not on when the generation occurred (PJM-GATS 2011c). Recently, due the decline in spot pricing, PJM-GATS has reported higher solar weighted average prices than the spot prices reported by SRECTrade and Flett Exchange. For example, if a company contracted for SRECs that were generated in January 2010 at a given price but did not retire those SRECs until August of 2011, the January 2010 price would be reflected in PJM-GATS's August 2011 solar weighted average price report.

10-year SREC contract prices ranged from $280/MWh to $448/MWh, depending on the project size and timing of the solicitation (Table 10).

Table 10. New Jersey EDC Solicitation 10-Year Contract Pricing, 2011

RPS Reporting Year 2011	Solicitation 6 Small	Solicitation 6 Mid-Sized	Solicitation 6 Large	Solicitation 7 Small	Solicitation 7 Mid-Sized	Solicitation 7 Large
Date bids submitted	2/17/11	2/17/11	2/17/11	6/10/11	6/10/11	6/10/11
Number of bids submit (participation)	86	78	27	83	115	29
Contracts awarded	59	35	12	35	19	9
Total capacity awarded (kW)	778	7,557	8,231	693	9,170	9,512
Average size (kW)	13	216	686	20	483	1,057
Average Net Present Value for contracts ($/kW)	$3,166*		$2,926	$2,683	$2,145	$1,983
Corresponding 10-yr renewable energy credit contract price ($/MWh)	$448*		$414	$379	$303	$280
Lowest Net Present Value ($/kW)	$2,819*		$2,424	$2,248	$1,759	$1,774
Corresponding 10-yr renewable energy credit contract price ($/MWh)	$399*		$343	$318	$249	$251

*In earlier solicitations, small and mid-sized projects were not solicited separately. The BPU's Solicitation 6 report does not distinguish between average SREC price for small and mid-sized projects.
Source: NJ BPU 2011a; NJ BPU 2011b

In Pennsylvania, SREC spot prices dropped to less than $50/MWh in September 2011 from approximately $300/MWh in mid-2010 (FlettExchange 2011), presumably due to oversupply in the market. Long-term (8.5 to 10.0 years) SREC contracts held by EDCs in Pennsylvania have seen prices ranging from $149/MWh to $286/MWh, as evidenced by prices from contracts solicited in February, May, and June 2011 (Table 11).

Table 11. Pennsylvania EDC Solicitation Contract Pricing, 2010–2011

EDC	Date of Solicitation(s)	Delivery Period	Total SREC Volume	Average Price/ SREC
Met-Ed/Penelec	Feb & June 2010	10 years	Feb: 10,000, June: 15,000	$286/MWh
Penn Power	Feb 2011	9 years	19,800	$199/MWh
PPL Electric	May 2011	8.5 years	25,500	$149/MWh
PPL Electric	June 2011	9 years	1,000	$149/MWh*

Sources: First Energy Corporation 2011a; First Energy Corporation 2011b; PPL Electric 2011a; PPL Electric 2011b
*Pricing was determined by the results of the May 2011 solicitation

In Washington, D.C., prices have declined as SRECs from other states have saturated the D.C. market. In 2010, SREC spot prices were closing between $200/MWh and $300/MWh, whereas in mid-2011, SREC spot prices dropped to between $50/MWh and $80/MWh. The Council of the District of Columbia addressed these issues by closing the door to most new out-of-district resources (current out-of-district resources will be grandfathered in) and increasing the ultimate solar requirement from 0.4% to 2.5% by 2023.

3.5 Compliance in SREC Markets
Compliance has Proved Challenging in Some SREC Markets, but Improved Compliance is Expected in Some Markets as Indicated by Price Drops and Installation Trends

The relatively high SREC prices in recent years, in many cases near the levels of solar ACPs, reflect the fact that some states have struggled with solar carve out compliance. However, the substantial drop in forward prices of SRECs in most states indicates that compliance challenges are dissipating and that markets may be oversupplied in some instances.

The largest shortfalls historically have been seen in New Jersey, which has by far the largest requirement. New Jersey experienced a large shortfall in 2009, with utilities paying about $39 million in solar ACPs (Figure 13). In 2010, the shortfall was slightly less, though still substantial, at $33 million. Recently, solar installations in New Jersey have surged, indicating that New Jersey will see fewer shortages in upcoming compliance periods.

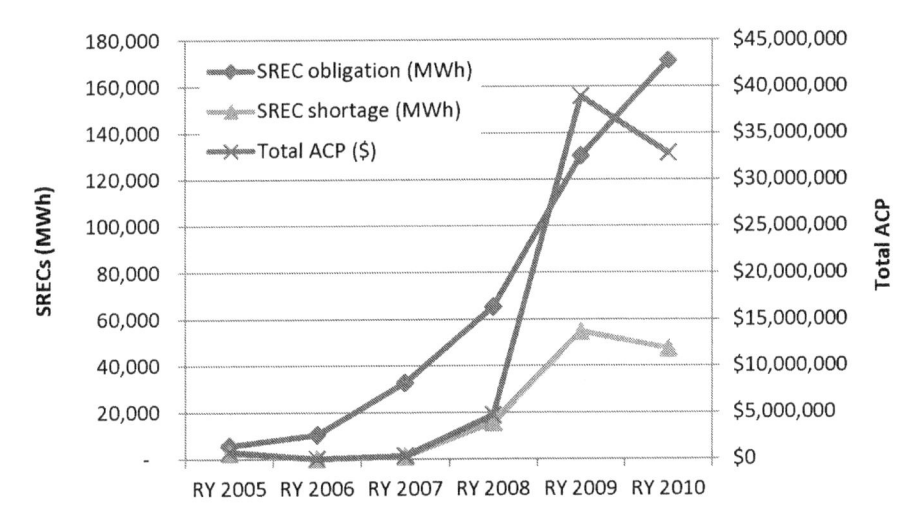

Figure 13. New Jersey solar carve out compliance

Note: RY stands for reporting year.

Maryland, Ohio, and Washington, D.C., have experienced shortages in SREC compliance in recent years, though compliance is looking more likely for 2010 and 2011 based on price trends in these markets. In Washington, D.C., future compliance is more difficult to predict, given the recent change in the compliance requirement. Table 12 shows compliance shortages and solar ACP payments in states with SREC targets in 2009 or earlier. In Pennsylvania, compliance has been nearly 100%, with one supplier choosing to pay the ACP for two SRECs in 2008. Shortages are unlikely in the future due to the pace of installations in the state.

Table 12. State Solar Carve Out Compliance, 2007–2009

	2007 SRECs required (MWh)	2007 SREC shortage (MWh)	2007 Total solar ACP ($1,000)	2008 SRECs required (MWh)	2008 SREC shortage (MWh)	2008 Total solar ACP ($1,000)	2009 SRECs required (MWh)	2009 SREC shortage (MWh)	2009 Total solar ACP ($1,000)
DC	N/A	N/A	N/A	900	146	$36	1,091	65	$18
DE	592	592	$178	1,225	1,225	$377	2,235	851	$426
MD	N/A	N/A	N/A	2,934	2,707	$1,218	6,125	2,865	$1,147
OH	N/A	N/A	N/A	N/A	N/A	N/A	3,955	2,858*	None**
PA	26	0	0	348	2	Not reported	1,221	-	None

*The total number of SRECs retired in Ohio is unknown because compliance reports by Competitive Retail Electric Service are deemed confidential. The figures here represent only the publicly available information provided by Ohio's Electric Distribution Utilities. The Ohio PUC estimated that 5,598 SRECs would be required in 2009 for the entire market.
**The Ohio PUC approved force majeure petitions by utilities, did not assess financial penalties, and added 2009 shortages to the 2010 obligation.
Note: Massachusetts and North Carolina began compliance in 2010. Missouri does not have a compliance obligation until 2011.

Maryland experienced shortfalls in 2008 and 2009, which was largely due to a shortage in supply. The 2008 Maryland SREC requirement was approximately 3,000, but only 276 SRECs were generated in 2008. Similarly, approximately 6,000 SRECs were needed to meet Maryland's 2009 requirement, but only 3,495 were generated. In 2008, Maryland utilities were short by 2,707 MWh and paid approximately $1,218,000 in solar ACPs. The shortage continued in 2009 when Maryland utilities were short by 2,865 MWh and paid $1,147,000 in solar ACPs.

In Washington, D.C., utilities did not submit any SRECs for compliance in 2007 or 2008. This resulted in shortages of 592 MWh in 2007 and 1,255 MWh in 2008, requiring solar ACPs totaling $178,000 and $377,000, respectively. In 2009, utilities continued to be short, this time by 851 MWh, resulting in $426,000 in solar ACPs.

In Ohio, utilities and competitive suppliers were unable to meet the in-state solar carve out requirement in 2009 but successfully petitioned to have the in-state solar requirement reduced for that year due to *force majeure*. In Ohio, the RPS includes a *force majeure* provision that enables obligated entities to request commission action in the event of an unforeseen circumstance outside of their control. In Ohio, utilities and competitive providers have stated that they made efforts to secure in-state solar SRECs but were not able to obtain enough SRECs through that process. FirstEnergy, the parent company of three Ohio utilities, also offered a residential SREC purchase program but was only able to procure 13 SRECs through the program in 2009 (Ohio Edison Company et al. 2010). Preliminary compliance reports have been issued in Ohio, while some utilities and competitive providers filed for *force majeure* in 2009. In 2010, most of the filers for *force majeure* were competitive providers and represented smaller volumes than 2009 (Siegfried 2011).

New Hampshire's first compliance year for its solar carve out was 2010. In 2010, entities paid $58,884 in ACPs (NH PUC 2011). At a solar ACP level of $160/MWh for 2010, the payment represents a shortage of 368 SRECs, or 8% of the total obligation of 4,255 SRECs (Epsen 2011).

Data from Massachusetts, Missouri, and North Carolina are not yet available because North Carolina and Massachusetts began compliance in 2010, and Missouri's first compliance year is 2011. Preliminary data indicate that a large shortage exists in Massachusetts (which had its first compliance year in 2010). Data from NEPOOL GIS indicate that only 2,738 MWh of qualifying Massachusetts solar were issued in 2010, compared to a requirement of approximately 34,000 MWh (Massachusetts DOER 2011c). The gap between installations and the requirement helps explain why Massachusetts SREC prices have not fallen as they have in other state markets.

Missouri's first compliance year is 2011 but is not expected to see shortages due to the ability of utilities to obtain SRECs from the national market. Similarly, in North Carolina, which had its first compliance year in 2010, utilities are expected to meet their solar requirements. SRECs can be banked for an unlimited amount of time in North Carolina and 25% of the SRECs can be procured nationally. One large IOU, Duke Energy, projects that it has contracts in place for a sufficient number of SRECs to meet its solar requirements through 2018 (NCUC 2011b).

4 Future Outlook

Looking forward, SREC markets are expected to continue to expand as state solar requirements ramp up over time from more than 520 MW$_{AC}$ in 2011 to approximately 2,000 MW$_{AC}$ by 2015 and 4,300 MW$_{AC}$ by 2020.

While several states struggled to achieve compliance recently, some markets show signs of improvement. A sharp drop in SREC prices in several states indicates that the markets may be oversupplied and on track to achieve near-term compliance targets. For example, energy year 2012 SREC spot pricing in New Jersey is at about $150/MWh compared to energy year 2011 spot market prices of more than $600/MWh. SREC prices have also eased in Pennsylvania. Other markets, such as Massachusetts, may continue to face shortages in the near term as its standard ramps up.

Substantial increases in installed capacity have been fueled by a 30% drop in module prices in the last year as well as slower growth in international markets that have placed greater emphasis on U.S. markets. While module prices declined from $2.21/W in the first quarter (Q1) of 2010 to $1.56/W, in Q2 2011, installed costs have not fully reflected these cost reductions yet, particularly in the residential market segment (SEIA GTM 2011a; SEIA GTM 2011b). Solar Energy Industries Association and Greentech Media report an approximate $0.50/W drop in residential installed PV costs nationally from the beginning of 2010 through Q2 2011 and more than $1.15/W drop in non-residential installed costs nationally over the same period (see Figure 14). Going forward, module cost reductions are likely to contribute to additional drops in installed costs. Given the drop in SREC prices in a number of markets, there will be increased pressure to drop installation prices to offset reduced revenue streams (SEIA GTM 2011b).

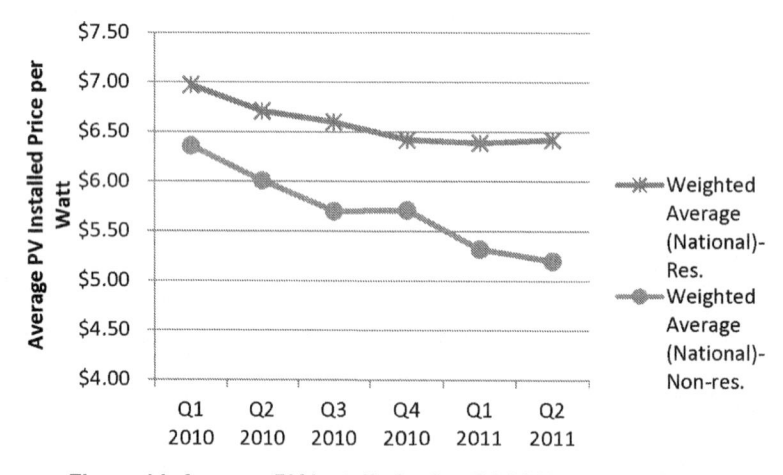

Figure 14. Average PV installed price Q1 2010 through Q2 2011

Sources: SEIA GTM 2011a; SEIA GTM 2011b

The current pace of project development is also influenced by the rapidly approaching expiration date of the Federal Treasury 1603 cash grant program, currently set to expire at the end of 2011. For projects to be eligible for the cash grants, they must meet safe harbor rules for commencing construction before the end of 2011, although completion is not required until 2016. Once the cash grant program expires, large projects in particular may require tax equity investors in order for the project to monetize the investment tax credit. The rate of development going forward will be influenced by the availability of tax equity and whether it will keep up with project demand. Also, the elimination of the cash grants may mean that developers place even greater emphasis on long-term contracts for SRECs to obtain debt financing for projects; thus, the continued availability of long-term contracting provisions or price floors will continue to be important.

Going forward, the increase in utility-scale PV projects may impact the supply and demand balance in state SREC markets, particularly those with relatively small carve outs. Large projects have the potential to achieve significant portions of the solar targets, which could result in rapid reductions in SREC prices. These effects may be particularly prevalent in some markets where large-scale projects have been planned, such as New Jersey, Ohio, and Maryland.

In New Jersey, the substantial uptick in installations in 2010 and the first half of 2011 are expected to keep the market in oversupply in the near term. Figure 15 shows the monthly trends in PV capacity installations in New Jersey. SRECTrade estimates that the average capacity required to meet the 2012 target is 370 MW, meaning that over the 2012 energy year, an average of 370 MW would need to be operating (SRECTrade 2011d). As of August 31, 2011, New Jersey had 430 MW installed (NJ OCE 2011). In addition to the current capacity expansion, the number of projects registered in New Jersey increased from just over 900 approved registrations at the end of August 2010 to over 3,700 approved projects by the end of July 2011 (representing over 430 MW) (NJ BPU 2011c).[13] While not all of these projects will ultimately be built, the backlog in registrations indicates that there is a potential for oversupply going forward in the New Jersey SREC market. As a result of recent installations and the existing project queue, industry analysts expect that the New Jersey market will be oversupplied through 2012 but may pick up again in 2013 (SEIA GTM 2011b).

Maryland had 42 MW installed at the end of Q2 2011 and 10.8 MW installed in the first half of 2011 alone, which industry analysts attribute to the newly available residential solar lease (SEIA GTM 2011b). Residential solar rebates are also available from the state. At least two large projects (>15 MW) are expected to begin commercial operation in Maryland in 2012, which would also play a substantial role in helping the state meet its compliance targets. However, it is unclear how the Maryland market will react when it is closed to out-of-state SRECs in 2012, but this will provide a boost for in-state projects.

In Pennsylvania, installations remained strong in the first half of 2011 due to significant project backlogs, despite an earlier drop in SREC prices. As of the first half of 2011, 105 MW had been installed, which is well ahead of current targets (SEIA GTM 2011b).

---

[13] These figures do not include completed projects.

Declining PV installation costs may have played a role in the uptick in installations; from Q2 2010 to Q2 2011, residential installation prices in Pennsylvania have declined from $7.13/W to $5.94/W, and non-residential installation prices have decreased over the same period from $6.23/W to $5.17/W (SEIA GTM 2011b). The market is expected to slow in the near term but could recover in 2013, perhaps in part to serve markets such as Illinois (SEIA GTM 2011b).

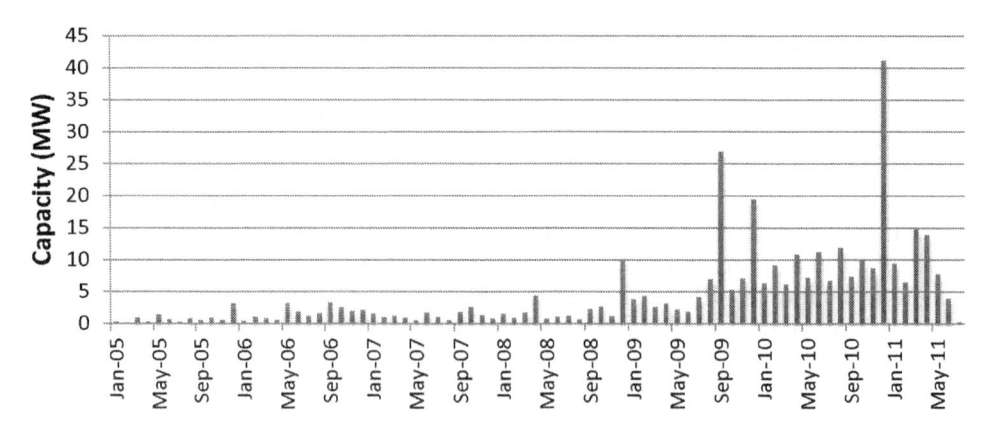

Figure 15. Capacity installed by month in New Jersey

Source: PJM-GATS 2011b

Recent legislative changes will have an impact on markets going forward. While most recent changes have resulted in stronger SREC targets, the uncertainty created by evolving policies can be a barrier to project development. Policymakers in Washington, D.C., and Connecticut have strengthened solar polices, while Massachusetts faced some criticism by solar developers for decreasing the solar ACP. In August 2011, Washington, D.C., policymakers expanded the solar requirement from 0.4% by 2020 to 2.5% by 2023 and specified that it be met by systems no larger than 5 MW and generally sited within D.C. In Connecticut, legislation (Bill 1243) was recently adopted requiring distribution companies to procure RECs from facilities <1 MW, spending $8 million in the first year and increasing by that same amount annually to $32 million in the fourth year. The companies must solicit 15-year contracts from small, mid-sized, and large facilities up to 1 MW. Finally, Massachusetts recently lowered its solar ACP from $600/MWh to $550/MWh and has proposed a long-term schedule reducing solar ACPs by 5% annually from 2013 to 2021, which helps provide certainty to the market for forward pricing.

Other state legislatures have recently considered bills to expand state solar carve outs, although none of these provisions have passed to date. In New Jersey, the Senate passed S2371, which would increase the SREC requirement in 2013 from 596 GWh to 772 GWh (the current 2014 requirement), with each subsequent annual requirement moving forward one year. In Pennsylvania, amendments (HB 1580) to the original RPS Act were introduced that would restrict solar eligibility to in-state resources and would increase the requirements for 2013–2015 compliance years from approximately 70 MW in 2013 to 207 MW in 2015 (SRECTrade 2011e). The New York legislature considered a bill this year to establish a solar carve out with an initial compliance requirement of 0.15% in 2012.

5 Summary and Conclusions

SREC markets have been implemented by a number of states to help encourage the development of solar energy systems and to facilitate compliance with state RPS solar carve outs. These markets are relatively new with some markets just beginning to operate while others have had several years of implementation experience. This report documents early experience with the design and implementation of SRECs markets. The key findings of this report are the following:

- *SREC markets are expected to grow rapidly in coming years as state solar requirements ramp up.* Of the 10 jurisdictions that allow and anticipate the use of SREC trading, the solar carve outs are scheduled to grow from more than 520 MW_{AC} in 2011 to nearly 7,300 MW_{AC} in 2025. Targets for solar generation vary from 0.2% to 3.5% of retail electric sales. SREC markets are dominated by PV, although solar thermal is eligible to meet solar requirements in a number of states.

- *Several states limit eligibility to in-state development, while a few allow SRECs from a broader geographic region.* Two jurisdictions—Washington, D.C., and Maryland—recently strengthened their in-state requirements, which will affect future development. A small national market for SRECs has resulted from solar requirements in North Carolina and Missouri that allow SRECs to be sourced from anywhere in the United States.

- *Solar ACPs are scheduled to decline over time reflecting expectations of declining PV costs.* Solar ACPs can be significant because they reflect the ceiling on SREC prices, and in shortage situations, SRECs typically trade near the solar ACP. New Jersey has had the highest solar ACP initially set at $700/MWh, but it is scheduled to be reduced to $600/MWh by 2015. Other state solar ACPs are scheduled to range from $300–$500/MWh by 2015.

- *New Jersey has been the dominant SREC market to date, but SREC markets in other states are expanding.* New Jersey has dominated because it has the earliest and largest solar requirement (more than four times larger than any other state). Additionally, the high New Jersey solar ACP has driven SREC prices to be the highest in the nation in recent years. However, SREC requirements in other states are growing, and projects are being implemented in a broader region. Voluntary markets for SRECs have been very limited given the substantial price differential between SRECs and RECs sourced from other technologies.

- *SREC spot prices have eased recently in a number of markets as installations have surged and compliance challenges have eased.* SREC prices have ranged from about $400–$650/MWh in New Jersey and about $200–$500/MWh in other states in recent years. In August 2011, spot prices for energy year 2012 SRECs in New Jersey dropped to $150/MWh compared to $500/MWh in May 2011. Pennsylvania energy year 2011 spot prices fell to about $50/MWh in August 2011 as a result of oversupply in the market. Similarly, in Washington, D.C., SREC spot prices dropped to $50–$80/MWh in summer 2011 from $200–$300/MWh in 2010 because out-of-district SRECs were allowed. In response, Washington,

D.C., adopted legislation generally restricting eligibility to in-district systems and expanded the solar targets substantially to reduce excess supply. A number of other states have introduced legislation that would expand the markets, but to date, no other legislation has passed.

- ***SREC markets are supporting a mix of PV system sizes, including residential and small to large commercial systems.*** In most markets, about two-thirds of registered projects are <10 kW. Projects >250 kW dominate capacity installed in a few markets, including North Carolina, Massachusetts, and New Jersey. There has been a trend toward large-sized projects recently, with the average size system in PJM exceeding 750 kW in the last few years.

- ***Installation of large systems could significantly impact compliance levels and prices.*** Large projects planned for New Jersey, Ohio, Maryland, and perhaps other states could impact prices and compliance levels. Only Massachusetts and Washington, D.C., currently cap the size of systems that can generate SRECs.

- ***Compliance has proved challenging in a number of SREC markets in recent years, but adequate supplies are expected going forward in many of these regions.*** A handful of states reported compliance shortfalls in 2009. The first compliance periods for a few markets occurred in 2010 or 2011. However, compliance challenges have eased in a number of markets recently, as evidenced by substantial declines in SREC prices. Surges in the rates of installations in New Jersey and Pennsylvania in particular have placed those states ahead of targets.

- ***Lack of long-term contracts has been a barrier to project developers obtaining financing in some markets.*** Several states have instituted long-term contracting requirements, price floors, or other provisions to try to overcome these challenges. The New Jersey program in particular has led to a greater number of long-term contracts, which has facilitated project development. However, the drop in SREC prices may mean that ratepayers must make up the difference between spot and contract prices. The price floor mechanism in Massachusetts has not been fully tested, but investors appear to be gaining comfort with this mechanism. The need for long-term contracting may continue to pose a problem, particularly in areas where rebates or other supplemental incentives expire and SRECs become the primary incentive stream for financing systems.

- ***Rate caps exist in some form in five SREC markets but have not been reached or are yet to be evaluated.*** The modest size of most solar carve outs suggests that it is not likely that rate caps will be reached in the near term.

References

AEP Ohio. (2011). Ohio Power Company Renewable Energy Technology Program Rider, PUCO #19. Issued June 22. https://www.aepohio.com/global/utilities/lib/docs/save/renewable/RETP_Rider.pdf. Accessed August 15, 2011.

Ameren Missouri. (2011a). "Standard Offer Contract." http://www.ameren.com/sites/aue/Environment/Renewables/Pages/StandardOfferContract.aspx. Accessed August 10, 2011.

Ameren Missouri. (2011b). "Renewable Energy Standard Compliance Plan 2011–2013." https://www.efis.psc.mo.gov/mpsc/. Accessed August 15, 2011.

Barbose, G. (October 31, 2011). Email. Lawrence Berkeley National Laboratory, Berkeley, CA.

Bernstein, H.; Judge, M.; Andrews, N. (14 July 2011). Personal communication. Massachusetts PUC and Massachusetts Department of Energy Resources, Boston, MA.

Bingaman, B. (2010). "Re: Policy Statement in Support of Pennsylvania Solar Projects Docket No. M-2009-2140263." www.puc.state.pa.us/pcdocs/1070428.pdf. Accessed August 3, 2011.

Bowery, B. (3 November 2011). Personal communication. SREC Trade, San Francisco, CA.

California Public Utilities Commission (CPUC). (7 October 2011). "Decision Implementing Portfolio Content Categories for the Renewables Portfolio Standard Program." Proposed decision 11-05-005. http://docs.cpuc.ca.gov/efile/PD/144972.pdf. Accessed November 3, 2011.

CPUC. (2011). "California Solar Initiative (CSI) Progress Report." Q2, Data Annex. http://www.cpuc.ca.gov/PUC/energy/Solar/legreports.htm. Accessed September 30, 2011.

Council of the District of Columbia. (2011). Distributed Generation Amendment Act of 2011, Permanent Legislation. http://www.dccouncil.washington.dc.us/images/00001/20110726120857.pdf. Accessed November 2, 2011.

Database of State Incentives for Renewables and Efficiency (DSIRE). (2011a). "Rules, Regulations & Policies." http://dsireusa.org/incentives/index.cfm?EE=1&RE=1&SPV=0&ST=0&searchtype=RPS&sh=1. Accessed October 3, 2011.

DSIRE. (2011b). "Maryland Public Service Commission—Solar Renewable Energy Certificates (SRECs)." http://dsireusa.org/incentives/incentive.cfm?Incentive_Code=MD55F&re=1&ee=1. Accessed August 3, 2011.

DSIRE. (2011c). "Ohio SREC-Based Financing Programs." http://www.dsireusa.org/incentives/incentive.cfm?Incentive_Code=OH61F&re=1&ee=1. Accessed August 15, 2011.

DSIRE. (2011d). "New Jersey Board of Public Utilities—Solar Renewable Energy Certificates (SRECs)." http://dsireusa.org/incentives/incentive.cfm?Incentive_Code=NJ07F&re=1&ee=1. Accessed August 3, 2011.

DSIRE. (2011e). "PSE&G – Solar Loan Program." http://dsireusa.org/incentives/incentive.cfm?Incentive_Code=NJ21F&re=1&ee=1. Accessed August 3, 2011.

Duke Energy Carolinas. (2011a). "Duke Energy Carolinas Standard Purchase Offer for Renewable Energy Certificates ('RECs')." http://www.duke-energy.com/pdfs/REC-Purchase-Offer-Info.pdf. Accessed August 15, 2011.

Duke Energy Carolinas. (2011b). "Duke Energy's 2010 REPS Compliance Report and Application for Approval of REPS Cost Recovery." E-7 Sub 984. http://ncuc.commerce.state.nc.us/cgi-bin/fldrdocs.ndm/INPUT?compdesc=Duke%20Energy%20Carolinas%2C%20LLC&numret=065&comptype=E&docknumb=7&suffix1=&subNumb=984&suffix2=&parm1=000135096. Accessed September 12, 2011.

Duke Energy Carolinas. (2011c). "Docket No. E-7, Sub 856, 2010 Annual Cost Update." http://ncuc.commerce.state.nc.us/cgi-bin/fldrdocs.ndm/INPUT?compdesc=Duke%20Energy%20Carolinas%2C%20LLC&numret=001&comptype=E&docknumb=7&suffix1=&subNumb=856&suffix2=&parm1=000128896. Accessed September 12, 2011.

Duke Energy Ohio. (2011). "Solar Renewable Energy Credits Program." http://www.duke-energy.com/ohio/renewable-energy/srec.asp. Accessed August 15, 2011.

Elefant, C.; Holt, E. (2011). *The Commerce Clause and Implications for State Renewable Portfolio Standard Programs*. Clean Energy States Alliance. http://www.cleanenergystates.org/resource-library/resource/cesa-report-the-commerce-clause-and-implications-for-state-renewable-portfolio-standard-programs-pdf. Accessed August 15, 2011.

Epsen, K. (2 November 2011). Email. New Hampshire Public Utilities Commission, Dover, New Hampshire.

First Energy Corporation. (2011a). "FAQ—Rules." https://www.firstenergycorp.com/utilitypowerprocurements/pa/srec/files/Penn_Power_Documents/GENERAL_FAQ-_PP_Solar_RFP-2011-02-24.pdf. Accessed August 3, 2011.

First Energy Corporation. (2011b). "Pennsylvania Power Company Completes Purchase of Solar Renewable Energy Credits press release 3-21-11." https://www.firstenergycorp.com/utilitypowerprocurements/pa/srec/files/Penn_Power_Documents/2011-03-18_Pennsylvania_Power_Company_Completes_Purchase_of_.pdf. Accessed August 3, 2011.

FlettExchange. (2011). Settlement Price. http://www.flettexchange.com/. Accessed October 3, 2011.

Flynn, H.; Breger, D.; Belden, A.; Bier, A.; Laurent, C.; Andrews, N.; Rickerson, W. (2010). "System Dynamics Modeling of the Massachusetts SREC Market." *Journal of Sustainability* (2); pp. 2746–2761.

Hart, D.M. (2010). "Making, Breaking, and (Partially) Remaking Markets: State Regulation and Photovoltaic Electricity in New Jersey." *Energy Policy* (38); pp. 6662–6673.

Heeter, J.; Bird, L. (2011). *Status and Trends in U.S. Compliance and Voluntary Renewable Energy Certificate Markets (2010 Data)*. Golden, CO: National Renewable Energy Laboratory.

Kansas City Power & Light (KCP&L). (2011). "2011 Annual Renewable Energy Standard Compliance Plan." Case No. EO-2011-0277. https://www.efis.psc.mo.gov/mpsc/. Accessed September 12, 2011.

Kansas City Power & Light General Missouri Operations (KCP&L-GMO). (2011). "2011 Annual Renewable Energy Standard Compliance Plan." Case No. EO-2011-0278. https://www.efis.psc.mo.gov/mpsc/. Accessed September 12, 2011.

Massachusetts Department of Energy Resources (Massachusetts DOER). (2011a). "Metering, Data Reporting, and Verification Requirements." http://www.mass.gov/?pageID=eoeeaterminal&L=5&L0=Home&L1=Energy%2c+Utilities+%26+Clean+Technologies&L2=Renewable+Energy&L3=Solar&L4=RPS+Solar+Carve-Out&sid=Eoeea&b=terminalcontent&f=doer_renewables_solar_metering-data-reporting&csid=Eoeea. Accessed October 3, 2011.

Massachusetts DOER. (2011b). "RPS Solar Carve-Out Qualified Units." http://www.mass.gov/Eoeea/docs/doer/rps_aps/solar-carve-out-units.xls. Accessed November 1, 2011.

Massachusetts DOER. (2011c). "Current Status of the RPS Solar Carve-Out Program." http://www.mass.gov/?pageID=eoeeamodulechunk&L=5&L0=Home&L1=Energy%2c+Utilities+%26+Clean+Technologies&L2=Renewable+Energy&L3=Solar&L4=RPS+Solar+Carve-Out&sid=Eoeea&b=terminalcontent&f=doer_renewables_solar_current-parameters&csid=Eoeea. Accessed September 30, 2011.

Massachusetts DOER. (2011d). "Solar Credit Clearinghouse Auction." http://www.mass.gov/?pageID=eoeeaterminal&L=5&L0=Home&L1=Energy%2c+Utilities+%26+Clean+Technologies&L2=Renewable+Energy&L3=Solar&L4=RPS+Solar+Carve-Out&sid=Eoeea&b=terminalcontent&f=doer_renewables_solar_solar-credit&csid=Eoeea. Accessed August 3, 2011.

Moore, G. (2011). "Utility Collaboration in Delaware's SREC Market." Presentation by Delmarva Power to Solar Power International, October 28, 2011.

Mosier, K. (10 August 2011). Personal communication. Maryland Public Service Commission, Baltimore, MD.

NERA Economic Consulting. (2011a). "NJ EDC Solar—Program Guide (July 18, 2011)." http://njedcsolar.com/documents.cfm. Accessed August 3, 2011.

NERA Economic Consulting. (2011b). "SREC-Based Financing Program Update." Available at: http://njedcsolar.com/assets/files/SREC-Based_Financing_Program_Update_7-28-111.pdf Accessed November 6, 2011.

New Hampshire Public Utilities Commission (NH PUC). (2011). "2010 Annual Compliance Report." http://www.puc.state.nh.us/Sustainable%20Energy/Renewable_Portfolio_Standard_Program.htm. Accessed November 2, 2011.

New Jersey Board of Public Utilities (NJ BPU). (2008). "NJ BPU Solar Financing Board Order." http://njcleanenergy.com/files/file/Board%20Orders/7-30-08-8E.pdf. Accessed August 3, 2011.

NJ BPU. (2011a). "Board Order Approving Results of the Sixth Solicitation (March 30, 2011)." http://njedcsolar.com/documents.cfm. Accessed August 3, 2011.

NJ BPU. (2011b). "Board Order Approving Results of the Seventh Solicitation (July 14, 2011)." http://njedcsolar.com/documents.cfm. Accessed August 3, 2011.

NJ BPU. (2011c). "SREC Registration Program Status Reports." http://www.njcleanenergy.com/renewable-energy/program-activity-reports/program-status-reports/srec-registration-program-status-reports. Accessed September 30, 2011.

NJ BPU. (2011d). "New Jersey's Renewable Portfolio Standard Rules: 2010 Annual Report." April 13, 2011 version. Available at: www.njcleanenergy.com/files/file/Renewable_Programs/Draft_2010_Annual_Report_for_New_Jersey_041311_version.pdf Accessed November 6, 2011.

NJ BPU. (2010). "Board Order Approving Results of the Fourth Solicitation (August 12, 2010)." http://njedcsolar.com/documents.cfm. Accessed August 3, 2011.

North Carolina Green Power (NCGP). (2011). "Become a Renewable Energy Generator." http://www.ncgreenpower.org/resources/. Accessed October 4, 2011.

North Carolina Utilities Commission (NCUC). (2011a). "NEW Renewable Energy Facility Registrations 2008–2011." www.ncuc.commerce.state.nc.us/reps/RegistrationSpreadsheet2008-2011.xls. Accessed November 1, 2011.

NCUC. (2011b). "Duke Energy Carolinas Application for Approval of Renewable Energy and Energy Efficiency Portfolio Standard Cost Recovery Rider, Docket E-7, Sub 984. Transcript of Testimony—Volume 1 (heard June 8, 2011), Cross-Examination by Mr. Olson of Kim Smith and Emily Felt." p. 87. http://ncuc.commerce.state.nc.us/cgi-bin/webview/senddoc.pgm?dispfmt=&itype=Q&authorization=&parm2=2BAAAA76111B&parm3=000135096. Accessed September 12, 2011.

Ohio Edison Company; Cleveland Electric Illuminating Company; Toledo Edison Company. (2010). "Annual Status Report and 2009 Compliance Review. Case No. 10-499-EL-ACP." http://dis.puc.state.oh.us/TiffToPDf/A1001001A10D15B51903F44369.pdf. Accessed October 3, 2011.

Pennsylvania PUC. (2011). "Final Policy Statement Order—Public Meeting of Sept. 16, 2010." http://www.puc.state.pa.us/electric/electric_alt_energy.aspx. Accessed August 3, 2011.

PJM-Generation Attribute Tracking System (PJM-GATS). (2011a). "RPS Retired Certificates (Reporting Year)." https://gats.pjm-eis.com/myModule/rpt/myrpt.asp?r=241&TabName=All. Accessed November 1, 2011.

PJM-GATS. (2011b). "Renewable Generators Registered in GATS." https://gats.pjm-eis.com/myModule/rpt/myrpt.asp?r=228. Accessed October 31, 2011.

PJM-GATS. (2011c). "Solar Weighted Average Price." https://gats.pjm-eis.com/myModule/rpt/myrpt.asp?r=230. Accessed October 3, 2011.

PPL Electric. (2011a). "Provider of Last Resort, AEPS. Solar Set-Aside Product." http://www.pplelectric.com/Business+Partners/polr-aeps-solar+set-aside+product/. Accessed August 3, 2011.

PPL Electric. (2011b). "Results of May 2011 Long Term Solar Solicitation." http://www.pplelectric.com/NR/rdonlyres/8A3D20E8-2BCC-4795-8992-1A24B57B872C/0/PAPUC_SecretarialLetter_17052011.pdf. Accessed August 3, 2011.

Progress Energy Carolinas. (2011a). "Application for Approval of REPS Cost Recovery Rider and Direct Testimony of Jay Foster." E-2 Sub 1000. http://ncuc.commerce.state.nc.us/cgi-bin/fldrdocs.ndm/INPUT?compdesc=PROGRESS%20ENERGY%20CAROLINAS%2C%20INC.%3B%20CAROLINA%20POWER%20%26%20LIGHT%20COMPANY%2C%20DBA&numret=065&comptype=E&docknumb=2&suffix1=&subNumb=1000&suffix2=&parm1=000135584. Accessed September 12, 2011.

Progress Energy Carolinas. (2011b). "Sunsense Solar PV Program." https://www.progress-energy.com/carolinas/business/save-energy-money/sunsense/commercial-solar-pv-program.page. Accessed August 15, 2011.

Public Service Commission of Maryland (PSC MD). (2011). "Renewable Energy Portfolio Standard Report of 2011, With Data for Compliance Year 2009." http://webapp.psc.state.md.us/intranet/Reports/MD%20RPS%202011%20Annual%20Report.pdf. Accessed October 4, 2011.

Sherwood, L. (2011). "U.S. Solar Market Trends 2010." Latham, New York: Interstate Renewable Energy Council. http://irecusa.org/wp-content/uploads/2011/07/IREC-Solar-Market-Trends-Report-revised070811.pdf. Accessed September 30, 2011.

Siegfried, S. (15 July 2011). Personal communication. Ohio Public Utilities Commission, Columbus, OH.

Solar Electric Power Association (SEPA). (2011). "Solar Data and Mapping Tool." http://www.solarelectricpower.org/solar-tools/solar-data-and-mapping-tool.aspx. Accessed October 4, 2011.

Solar Energy Industries Association (SEIA). (2011). "Utility-Scale Solar Projects in the United States Operating, Under Construction, or Under Development." www.seia.org/galleries/pdf/Major%20Solar%20Projects.pdf. Accessed September 30, 2011.

SEIA and GTM Research (GTM). (2011a). "U.S. Solar Market Insight: 2010 Year-In-Review."

SEIA and GTM. (2011b). "U.S. Solar Market Insight: 2nd Quarter 2011."

SEIA and GTM. (2011c). "U.S. Solar Market Insight: 1st Quarter 2011."

SRECTrade. (2011a). "State SREC Markets." http://www.srectrade.com/background.php. Accessed October 3 2011.

SRECTrade. (2011b). "50 MW Ohio Solar Project Secures Further Financing." http://www.srectrade.com/blog/srec-markets/50-mw-ohio-solar-project-secures-further-financing. Accessed October 3, 2011.

SRECTrade. (2011c). "SREC Market Prices." http://srectrade.com/srec_prices.php. Accessed October 4, 2011.

SRECTrade. (2011d). "New Jersey Installed Capacity Update." http://www.srectrade.com/blog/srec-markets/new-jersey-installed-capacity-update. Accessed October 3, 2011.

SRECTrade. (2011e). "Pennsylvania Legislature Commences Efforts to Fix SREC Program." http://www.srectrade.com/blog/srec-markets/pennsylvania/pennsylvania-legislature-commence-efforts-to-fix-srec-program. Accessed October 24, 2011.

Stewart, C. (22 July 2011). Personal communication. Delaware Public Service Commission, Dover, Delaware.

Tennessee Valley Authority (TVA). (2011). Generation Partners. http://www.tva.com/greenpowerswitch/partners/index.htm. Accessed October 4, 2011.

Union of Concerned Scientists (UCS). (2008). "Summary Information of State RPS Programs." www.ucsusa.org/assets/documents/clean_energy/pennsylvania.pdf. Accessed September 30, 2011.

Wiser, R.; Barbose, G.; Holt, E. (October 2010). *Supporting Solar Power in Renewable Portfolio Standards: Experience from the United States*. LBNL-3984E. Berkeley, CA: Lawrence Berkeley National Laboratory.

Appendix

Long-Term Contracting Provisions: SREC Auctions in New Jersey

In 2008, the New Jersey Board of Public Utilities (the "Board") established a three-year, long-term contracting program for SRECs for the state's regulated distribution utilities (NJBPU 2008). The program is called the SREC-Based Financing Program because these auctions are intended to help winning residential and commercial developers secure financing for their solar projects. The contracts resulting from the auctions are standardized and non-negotiable, and developers are encouraged to bid for SREC contracts that would provide sufficient project returns. The Board has included a provision that precludes a project that receives an award in one solicitation to compete in a future solicitation at a higher price absent a "clear indication of a change in circumstances" (NJ BPU 2010).

For RPS Reporting Years 2010–2012, Jersey Central Power and Light Company, Atlantic City Electric Company, and Rockland Electric Company are required to hold at least two auctions annually to select competitive proposals for SRECs under long-term contracts. To recover associated costs, the utilities are able to auction the SRECs procured in the SREC-Based Financing Program to the state's generation suppliers.

The auctions are held for SREC contracts between 10 and 15 years. This length enables solar projects to obtain financing and addresses a barrier to development. The bidder submits a pricing proposal ($/SREC and contract duration) and a summary of project qualifications (NERA Economic Consulting 2011a). Since bids may vary in terms, the auctioneer ranks each bid according to the net present value of payments under the SREC agreement. There is an undisclosed price limit when evaluating bids, and the auctioneer decides whether or not there are enough competitive bids to meet the auctioned quantity (NERA Economic Consulting 2011a).

The Board-mandated program has the goal of procuring more than 64 MW over three years: 42 MW for Jersey Central Power and Light Company, 19 MW for Atlantic City Electric Company, and 3.769 MW for Rockland Electric Company (NERA Economic Consulting 2011b). For each solicitation, the Board publishes a planned quantity/capacity cap for each EDC, and the auctioneer accepts bids in order of competitiveness up to that cap. If in a given solicitation the planned quantity is not procured, the Board assigns the shortfall to subsequent auctions. In RPS reporting years 2010 and 2011, the three EDCs procured a total of 47.5 MW in six separate solicitations. The remaining 16.5 MW of the total program target will be procured in two or three solicitations during the 2012 RPS reporting year (NERA Economic Consulting 2011b).

In 2010, the program expanded eligibility to residential and commercial programs up to 2 MW_{DC} in size, from the earlier 500 kW limit, to increase participation (NERA Economic Consulting 2011a). The program administrators consider three segments of project sizes: a small project size segment (<50 kW); a mid-size project segment (>50 kW, <500 kW); and a large project size segment (>500 kW, <2 MW).

Long-Term Contracting Provisions: Competitive Solicitations in Pennsylvania

In September 2010, the Pennsylvania PUC adopted a "Policy Statement in Support of Pennsylvania Solar Projects" (see PUC Code §69.2901-2903). The policy statement encourages EDCs to issue RFPs for large-scale solar projects (>200 kW) using a transparent and open competitive bidding process. The statement also suggests that EDCs can procure SRECs from small-scale projects (<200 kW) through both RFPs and bilateral contracts. The policy statement specifies that the price negotiated for SRECs from small-scale projects should not exceed the commission-approved average winning bid price in the EDC's most recent RFP for large-scale solar projects (Pennsylvania PUC 2011).

In response, Pennsylvania EDCs have started to hold competitive solicitations to procure a portion of their SREC obligations over a longer delivery period (e.g., 7–10 years). Four of Pennsylvania's 11 EDCs have held RFPs for long-term SREC contracts to date, including: Metropolitan Edison Company, Pennsylvania Electric Company, Pennsylvania Power Company, and PPL Electric Utilities.

The utilities have structured their procurements so that long-term contracts expire in 8–10 years (2020) when the Pennsylvania alternative energy portfolio standard concludes. The utilities are seeking bids in tranches (i.e., 100, 250, or 500 SRECs per year from an individual supplier). SREC suppliers have the responsibility of delivering the quantity of SRECs specified by their contract each year. One advantage of this approach is that the utility does not have to bear the risks associated with individual project performance (Bingaman 2010).

SREC Price Floor Programs: Massachusetts and New Jersey Utility PSE&G
Massachusetts Solar Credit Clearinghouse
In 2010, Massachusetts created the Solar Credit Clearinghouse Auction, which functions as a long-term price floor for SRECs in the Massachusetts market. Massachusetts opted for this approach because there was little appetite to adopt long-term contracting provisions at the time the solar carve out was implemented (Bernstein et al. 2011).

Under the clearinghouse program, the Massachusetts Department of Energy Resources (DOER) will hold an annual fixed-price SREC auction where generators can deposit eligible, unsold SRECs into an auction account with the NEPOOL-GIS. Solar generators may deposit SRECs into the account during the final 31 days of each compliance year's Q4 trading period (May 16–June 15). If any SRECs are deposited, DOER must hold an auction to clear these SRECs prior to July 31 of that year. Bidders submit the volume that they are willing to buy for the fixed price of $300/MWh, the floor price for the SRECs (Massachusetts DOER 2011d). There is a 5% auction fee, so generators will receive $285 for each SREC cleared on the auction (instead of $300/SREC).

At the time of qualification, generators will be given an "opt-in term," which signifies the number of quarters that their project will have the opportunity to deposit SRECs into the auction account. The opt-in term for new projects is currently 10 years. The opt-in term for future projects may be adjusted annually based on market conditions, but any adjustment will have no impact on projects that have already been qualified. If the SREC market is oversupplied, the DOER will decrease the opt-in period for new systems to temper market growth (Flynn et al. 2010). For every 10% of the compliance obligation met by deposits into the auction, the opt-in term will be reduced by one year. It will not decrease more than two years at a time. In the event of a shortage, the opt-in term will increase by one year for each 10% of the compliance obligation met through solar ACP payments. The opt-in term may never be longer than 10 years. It cannot decrease below five years until after 2016.

When SRECs are deposited into the auction account, they are re-minted with an initial shelf life of two years, meaning that they can be used for compliance for either one of the next two compliance years. The compliance obligation the following year is increased by the amount of SRECs deposited in the auction. If there is insufficient bid volume to clear the auction account SRECs, the shelf life is increased to three years, and the auction is repeated (Massachusetts DOER 2011d). If the second auction does not clear, a third and final auction will be held. SRECs retain the three-year shelf-life from the second auction, and the compliance obligation for the following year is increased a second time by the amount of SRECs in the auction account. If there are insufficient bids to clear this final auction, depositors will be paid on a pro-rated basis for the number of SRECs deposited relative to the number sold. Any remaining SRECs will be returned to depositors, who will have three years to sell them.

The auction is intended as a market of last resort. Once a SREC is moved into the auction account, it cannot be removed (Massachusetts DOER 2011d). The auction mechanism has not yet been used because there has been a shortage of SRECs to date.

PSE&G Solar Loan Program
The Public Service Electric & Gas Company (PSE&G) Solar Loan Program has elements of a long-term price floor. Under the program, PSE&G lends money to its retail customers to cover 40%–60% of the cost of a PV system. Customers may repay the loan principal and interest through cash payments or by signing their SRECs over to PSE&G. The loan term is 15 years, and during this period, PSE&G credits customers for each SREC generated according to market conditions but not below the established price floor. The price floor as of January 2011 is $420/SREC for residential borrowers and $380/SREC for commercial borrowers. The price floor declines over time; however, the floor price applicable at the time of loan closing remains in effect for a particular project for the entire duration of the loan (DSIRE 2011e). Customers will be paid at least the floor price for each SREC generated, but if trading prices are higher, customers may be paid more. PSE&G reserves the right to purchase SRECs generated by the system at 75% of the market price through the original term of the loan (DSIRE 2011e). The Solar Loan I program, which was initiated in 2008, had the goal of installing 30 MW of customer-sited PV. Solar Loan II, which began in December 2009, has a current program target of 51 MW of installed capacity (NJ BPU 2011d).

CPSIA information can be obtained
at www.ICGtesting.com
Printed in the USA
LVOW03s0211080916

503708LV00014B/116/P